East Fourth Street

The Rise, Decline, and Rebirth of an Urban Cleveland Street

Alan F. Dutka

PUBLISHING INFORMATION

Published by
Cleveland Landmarks Press, Inc.
13610 Shaker Boulevard, Suite 503
Cleveland, Ohio 44120-1592
www.clevelandlandmarkspress.com
(216) 658 4144

©2011, Cleveland Landmarks Press, Inc.
All Rights Reserved

ISBN--978-0-936760-30-8

LIBRARY OF CONGRESS CONTROL NUMBER
2011926629

Designed by
John Yasenosky, III

Printed by
Sheridan Books, Inc.
Chelsea, Michigan

Table Of Contents

Preface

In a book's preface, the author conveys his or her inspiration for devoting considerable time and effort to create a manuscript worthy of publication. Authors sometimes describe a lifelong desire to depict something especially significant or important to them. My motivation tended to be much less grandiose. The short version is I just thought the history of East Fourth Street would make a great story.

Born and raised in Cleveland, I drew my first breath in a hospital on Carnegie Avenue less than three miles from Fourth Street. Even as a college student, I never lived more than four miles from the narrow, short road. But I have no recollection of ever dining or shopping on Fourth Street until the 21st Century. In the 1960s, I often used the modest passageway as a shortcut from Euclid Avenue to Kay's Bookstore, one block south on Prospect Avenue. My most vivid memory of the street dates to 1994 when I accompanied a suburban couple to an event at the brand-new Gund Arena. I suggested using the two-block street as the most direct route from Euclid Avenue to the arena. The female member of the couple, after taking one look at Fourth Street, became so intimidated she refused to walk down the road.

Today I live eight short blocks from Fourth Street. As a downtown resident, I witnessed firsthand the amazing transformation that occurred during the past decade. I recall taking a tour of the Gateway area and listening to Nick Kostis describe his plans for an entertainment center in a building that, at the time, looked more appropriate for conducting military exercises in a simulated war zone. Two years later, Kostis's stunning Pickwick and Frolic complex opened to rave reviews.

As upscale venues continued to replace wig stores and pawn shops, I walked down the street speculating how the remarkable conversions occurred. These reflections inspired the research culminating in the publication of this book. I reconstructed the past using fragile old history books, what seemed to be miles of microfilm, and on-line search engines and references. I also talked with a wide variety of individuals who helped create the recent renaissance – planners, developers, entrepreneurs, and urban residents.

After conducting my final interview, Sean Bilovecky took me on a guided tour of the site that would become Dredgers Union. A pristine air conditioning unit sat next to a mound of rubble that must have accumulated over a period of decades. Sean confidently visualized a vintage-looking but brand new elevator in operation where a hefty heap of dust and dirt currently resided. New offices for designing trendy apparel would arise in a basement currently inhabited by rodents and spiders. As I walked back to my apartment, I realized I had finished the process almost exactly where it all started, more than a decade earlier, with Nick Kostis's presentation in the next-door building.

Although Kostis and Bilovecky are separated in age by almost two generations, the passion in their eyes and excitement in their voices appeared almost identical as they discussed their Fourth Street aspirations. A similar exhilaration pervades almost every planner, stakeholder, businessperson, and resident involved with the street's astonishing renaissance.

As an author, I hope I possess enough talent to portray this enthusiasm, so, as you read this book, you will heartily agree with my original premise: East Fourth Street makes a great story.

Alan F. Dutka
April 2011

Acknowledgments

More than 50 persons made significant contributions to the East Fourth Street story; some shared their memories while others provided pictures, important technical information, and outstanding research skills. The contributors include:

Bonfoey Gallery:
Olga Merela
Richard Moore
Dana Oldfather

Brandsetter Carroll Inc.:
Rick Parker

Chinato:
Sharon Bizga

City Of Cleveland:
Donald Petit (Landmarks Commission)

Cleveland Public Library:
Margaret Baughman (Photographs)
Aaron Mason (Business)
Sabrina Miranda (Microform Center)
Amy Pease (History)
Michael Ruffing (History)
Denise Sanders (Microform Center)
John Skrtic (Social Sciences)
Elmer Turner (Photographs)
Chris Wood (History)

Cleveland State University:
Lynn M. Duchez Bycko (Special Collections)

Cuyahoga Research Group:
John D. Cimperman

Dances With Walls:
James Todd

Dredgers Union:
Sean Bilovecky
Danielle DeBoe

Epstein Design Partners:
Maria Gutzwiller

Erie Island Coffee Shop:
Alan Glazen
Annalie Glazen
Martin Reuben

Flannery's Pub:
Christine Connell

Gateway Church:
Alex Ennes

Greenhouse Tavern:
Jonathon Sawyer

Historic Gateway Neighborhood Corp.:
Kelly Lange
Thomas Starinsky
Thomas Yablonsky

Historian:
Ralph Horner

John Blazy Designs:
John Blazy

La Strada:
Terry Tarantino

Lola:
Michael Symon
Rebecca Yody

Mariott:
Eddie Carter

MRN:
Ari Maron

Ohio Beauty College (graduate):
Maria Barile

Otto Moser's Restaurant:
Steve Dimotsis

ParkWorks:
Nancy Boylan

Pickwick & Frolick:
Nick Kostis
John Lorinee

Positively Cleveland:
Samantha Fryberger
Joyce Noss
April Prior

Saigon Restaurant:
Kenny Ho
Bon Thei

Sincere Building:
Nick Zarnes

Sisser Jewelry (and Fourth Street visionary):
Bob Zimmer

Five individuals provided invaluable assistance by suggesting changes, clarifications, and modifications, and by editing the manuscript and designing the layout of the book. My wife Priscilla Dutka and daughter Diane Dutka bore the brunt of offering excellent constructive comments after reading my initial drafts. Greg Deegan and Jim Toman of Cleveland Landmarks Press continued the process in their usual outstanding manner. John Yasenosky, created the book's beautiful design.

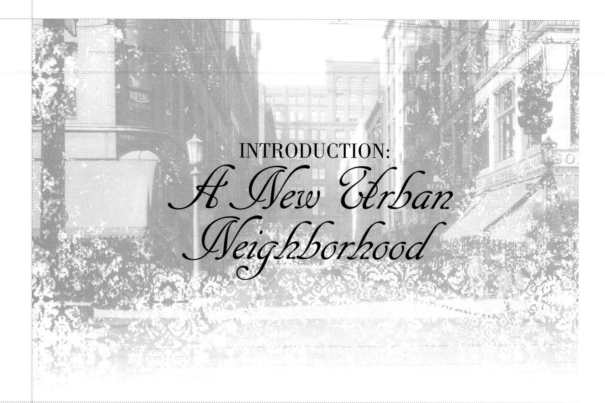

INTRODUCTION:
A New Urban Neighborhood

East Fourth Street is not much more than a glorified alley, a narrow walkway extending 450 feet between Euclid and Prospect avenues. The street and its 13 vintage buildings, crammed tightly together with little breathing room, occupy a space smaller than many suburban residential lots. Technically, Fourth Street continues south one additional block where a single restaurant thrives in an area otherwise consumed by parking lots. Yet this modest enclave is the hottest urban setting in the city. Its redevelopment is attracting widespread national attention, including complimentary articles in the *New York Times.*

The confined passageway, jam-packed with turn-of-the-century to 1920s buildings, contains 600,000-square-feet of historic redevelopment, one-third devoted to chic restaurants and entertainment

venues, while fashionable apartments and condominiums occupy the space above these urban hotspots. Fourth Street is a preferred choice for dining and drinking before or after sports events and concerts, a popular option for business lunches, and an entertainment haven for downtown residents, suburbanites, and tourists.

As a residential community, the neighborhood's amenities attract young professionals with almost magnetic powers. An urbanite living on Fourth Street might begin Sunday morning by savoring a freshly brewed cup of latte coffee before attending a Christian worship service. After enjoying lunch at one of a variety of excellent restaurants, the city dweller could practice making strikes and spares in a fashionable bowling alley. Before or after viewing a popular music concert or first-rate comedy club performance, a Fourth Street resident can enjoy dinner at a renowned restaurant. These varied activities, all accomplished on Fourth Street, are within a 450-foot walk of the urbanite's apartment or condominium.

A journey just one block south is all that is needed to witness a Cleveland Cavaliers basketball contest, professional hockey match, arena football competition, or major concert. A large shopping mall with additional dining choices is located five minutes to the west. The same distance to the east places a Fourth Street urbanite at a Cleveland Indians game or yet another set of restaurants and clubs. The third-largest performing arts center in the country is within a ten-minute easterly jaunt. To the north, the Cleveland Browns Stadium, the Rock and Roll Hall of Fame, and Great

Lakes Science Center are within walking distance. After enjoying an exciting Sunday, many Fourth Street residents take a leisurely five-minute Monday morning stroll to their workplaces. One tenant of the Windsor Block needs only two minutes to reach the Cleveland Public Library, his place of employment. The short walk across Euclid and Superior avenues, broken up by a pleasant stroll through the Old Arcade, rarely requires wearing a coat, even in Cleveland's coldest weather.

Downtown apartments traditionally attract a wide range of demographic groups, ranging from college students to retired persons, some of whom have lived in the same building for more than 35 years. Fourth Street, on the other hand,

The right edge of the photo shows the southern end of East Fourth Street, where it connects with Woodland Avenue. The huge Sheriff Street Market, recalling East Fourth's original name, lines the street's eastern edge. The new (1927) Ohio Bell Building on Huron Road is at the left of the view. *(Cleveland State University, Bruce Young Collection)*

noted for a preponderance of young urban professionals, is unique to downtown Cleveland. The short, narrow street, with its coffee shop, bar, and church, creates a distinctive sense of belonging, capturing the intimacy of old city neighborhoods. The combination of modern amenities and historically significant buildings generates an appeal especially attractive to younger residents.

Although a few empty-nesters enjoy Fourth Street's distinct atmosphere, apartment residents tend to be near 30 years in age. Many are rapidly rising business professionals, typified by a young vice president of a large construction company and an under-30 banker at Quicken Loans. The Sincere Building condominiums, initially purchased at an average cost of $320,000, appealed almost entirely to buyers in their early 30s. The group consisted of two bankers, a cello player in the Cleveland Orchestra, a physician, three attorneys, two mortgage brokers who later subleased the apartment to a pair of Cleveland Cavaliers, and a software company.

Yet, as late as 1997, the street consisted almost entirely of low-end retailing, vacant storefronts, and decaying buildings. The remarkable 21st-Century transformation is the most recent chapter in a story of change unfolding throughout Fourth Street's captivating two-century history.

Fourth Street's past contains fascinating tales of both triumphs and catastrophes. A veteran theater operator gambled his life savings to create Cleveland's most prestigious showplace, only to surrender his dream palace at a sheriff sale. A hard-working entrepreneur carefully nurtured a small market stand into an international corporation, while flames consumed the dreams of less fortunate merchants. An established storeowner proudly received a prestigious award for championing Fourth Street's revitalization, but closed his own business as a direct consequence of the street's rebirth.

These stories, along with a myriad of similar anecdotes, bestow life and character to the sidewalks, shops, and buildings comprising Fourth Street.

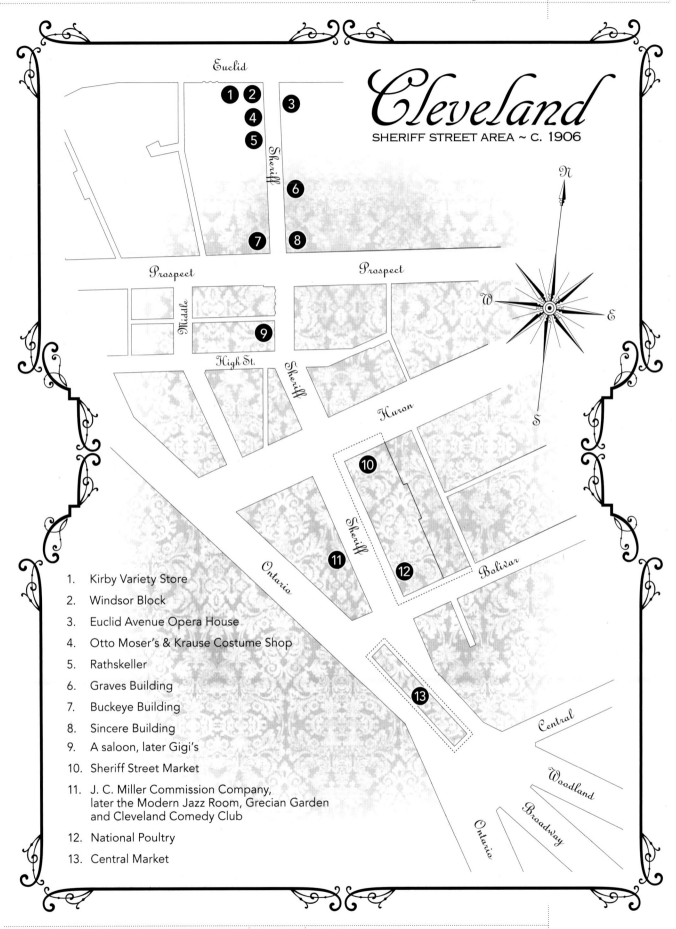

Cleveland
SHERIFF STREET AREA ~ C. 1906

1. Kirby Variety Store
2. Windsor Block
3. Euclid Avenue Opera House
4. Otto Moser's & Krause Costume Shop
5. Rathskeller
6. Graves Building
7. Buckeye Building
8. Sincere Building
9. A saloon, later Gigi's
10. Sheriff Street Market
11. J. C. Miller Commission Company, later the Modern Jazz Room, Grecian Garden and Cleveland Comedy Club
12. National Poultry
13. Central Market

Chapter I
From the Beginning

East Fourth Street's legacy actually began more than a generation before its formal existence. In the winter of 1809, Levi Johnson journeyed to Cleveland from Buffalo using a sleigh to navigate Lake Erie's frozen surface. In Cleveland, Johnson accumulated considerable wealth building homes, ships, and lighthouses. He also erected three structures comprising an almost full-service facility for the town's legal activities: a courthouse, jail, and gallows. In 1811, he built a log cabin for his family on a large parcel of land on the south side of Euclid Avenue, extending from Public Square to what would become Fourth Street. Using the surrounding dense forest as a source for wood, Johnson constructed ships on the site of the later Windsor Block, located on the corner of Euclid Avenue and Fourth Street. Oxen dragged the completed vessels on rollers down rutted Euclid and Superior avenues for launching in the Cuyahoga River. In 1814, 56 oxen combined to haul his 60-ton ship *Pilot* to the river. From this humble beginning,

Cleveland became a major center for shipbuilding.

Commercial Business Transforms a Residential Street (1835 – 1900)

Fourth Street's saga began in the 1830s when city planners designed the narrow connection between Euclid and Prospect avenues. A sheriff, the street's initial resident, inspired the name Sheriff Street. The label remained until 1906 when every Cleveland road running north and south disowned its original name to become a number. At that time, Sheriff Street assumed its current identify as East Fourth Street.

Elm trees eventually lined both sides of the alluring street filled with New York apartment-style homes and more modest, although still appealing, frame houses. This upper-class neighborhood never rivaled the later grandeur of Euclid Avenue's Millionaires Row, but its quiet, aristocratic appearance attracted many well-bred Cleveland families. The residential character, however, remained intact for less than two generations as business unrelentingly infringed on the once peaceful neighborhood street.

In 1837, architect Charles W. Heard constructed his family residence on Euclid Avenue, just east of Fourth Street. In time, Heard's architectural achievements greatly influenced the street's transition to a commercial thoroughfare. The first major encroachment on residential life occurred when Heard designed St. Paul's Episcopal Church, located on the southwest corner of Euclid Avenue and Fourth Street. The congregation purchased an 80-foot strip of land on Euclid Avenue and extending 120 feet down Fourth Street. The church paid $2,800 ($35 per foot) for the frontage. At the time, the property sat on an unpaved street lacking sidewalks. In 1849, fire destroyed the house of worship before it conducted its first service. A rebuilt church, completed in 1851, included a side entrance on Fourth Street, an architectural scheme later copied by several five-and-ten-cent chains. Less than a quarter century later, St. Paul's surrendered to business expansion. In 1874, construction of Silas Brainard's music store necessitated razing the church.

The four-story Brainard Building, erected in 1877 to house the Brainard music company, burned in 1908; the fire also destroyed the structure to the right. The current Windsor Block is composed of the building on the left, located on the corner of Euclid Avenue and Fourth Street, and the two buildings constructed to replace those destroyed by the fire. *(Alan Dutka collection)*

THE BRAINARD FAMILY:
FOURTH STREET'S MUSICAL PIONEERS

The Nathan Brainard family, consisting of 48-year-old Nathan, his 44-year-old wife Fanny, and their seven children, endured an arduous journey from New Hampshire to seek new opportunities in rapidly growing Cleveland. For 55 years after the family's arrival in 1834, members of four generations of Brainards lived or worked on Fourth Street.

The Brainards built their first home on the southeast corner of Prospect Avenue

and Fourth Street. A few years later, the family constructed a block of four brick homes on the later site of the McCrory variety store, directly south of a small orchard of peach trees, the present location of Pickwick & Frolic. Through the years, these residences accommodated the original nine Brainard settlers and their extended families headed by Nathan's four sons, Silas, Henry, George, and Joseph. Jabez Brainard, the elderly father of Nathan, joined his son and grandchildren in Cleveland after his wife died in 1846. He lived on Fourth Street until his death, at the age of 94, in 1852.

Nathan, a grocer by trade, founded a food business with Silas, his oldest son. Nathan also joined his partner Henry Mould in establishing a company, located on Fourth Street, to sell Chickering pianos. Silas, an accomplished flutist, nurtured a passion for music that greatly exceeded his interest in groceries, explaining his quick transfer to the more artistic of the two businesses. In 1840, Silas married Emily Mould, the daughter of the piano company's co-owner. Further intermixing family and business, Silas's brother Henry married Emily's sister Laura. Nathan's two other sons engaged in similar sets of marriages, Joseph marrying Helen Hills, and his brother George wedding Helen's sister Maria.

Under Silas's enthusiastic and savvy leadership, the piano company expanded to sell sheet music and other musical instruments. Silas began publishing *Western Musical World*, a monthly journal regarded as one of the country's leading music publications. Each edition, selling for 15 cents, contained musical news, articles, editorials, helpful hints to musicians, question-and-answer columns, sheet music selections, and biographical sketches. Renamed *Brainard's Musical World* in 1869, the journal continued publication until 1895.

In 1871, Silas died, at the age of 57. His sons, Charles and Henry, became the third generation of the family to own the business. In the 1870s and 1880s, the company gained a national reputation publishing vocal and instrumental music, songbooks, and political and patriotic songs. In 1877, the company moved to a new four-story building near the southwest corner of Euclid Avenue and Fourth Street. The interior contained the latest conveniences, including impressive woodwork, gas lights, and a steam-driven elevator. Just two years earlier, the neighboring Centennial Building (current W. T. Grant Lofts site) installed the first elevator in Cleveland. A local newspaper referred to the innovation as a "new fangled death trap known as an elevator."

The company expanded, establishing a Chicago office in 1878. Six years later, Henry founded his own business, serving as an agent for Steinway, Hazleton, and other first-class pianos. At the turn of the century, Henry added premium-priced bicycles to his company's offerings. Henry sold his business in 1906, later founding a new company to sell pianos and the latest technical wonder, the Victor talking machine. In 1889, Charles moved the original Brainard Company to Chicago, leaving no trace of the business in Cleveland.

Retail shops replaced the street-level portions of the old Brainard homes on Fourth Street, while the upper floors served as apartments. All of these buildings have since been razed or destroyed by fire. The Brainard headquarters on Euclid Avenue and Fourth Street burned in the 1908 Kirby dime store fire.

In the final quarter of the 19th Century, Fourth Street became a bustling mercantile road. In 1870, Charles Heard still lived in the home he built on Euclid Avenue more than three decades earlier, sharing the property with seven of his children and two servants. Heard sacrificed his residence to construct the commercial Heard Block containing an elegant side entrance to the Euclid Avenue Opera House, another of his celebrated architectural triumphs. The Opera House's main entrance fronted Fourth Street.

At the dawn of the 20th Century, retail tenants in the Heard Block included a pharmacy, florist shop, dentist, and cash-and-carry clothing store. The Opera House Pharmacy offered Liebig's malt extract (14 cents), Yankee rubber sponges (11 cents), hair insoles – a sure preventative against rheumatism (10 cents per pad), and antiseptic cream for chapped hands and face (25 cents).

The U. S. Dental Rooms examined and extracted teeth without charge. The extraction process used Veg-O-Zan, the company's specially formulated preparation to insure safe and painless results. Prices for other services included a good set of teeth ($5.00), bridge work ($4.00), a choice of fillings made of gold ($1.00 each) or other materials (50 cents each), and a selection of crowns using 24-k gold ($5.00) or less desirable substances ($3.00).

Charles Campbell, the veteran doorman at the Opera House, and a forerunner of the colorful personalities that would later contribute to Short

The Euclid Avenue Opera House dominated Fourth Street in the 1870s. A laundry is located in the former small residential home south of the Opera House. The Terrace Apartments, situated in another former residential house, are at the far right. *(Ralph Horner)*

Vincent's legacy, always wore a top hat as he walked down Fourth Street, morning or night, summer or winter. Another unusual character lived in the Opera House Pharmacy; a large cat with a gold tooth, who allowed visitors to open its mouth and inspect the incisor, although never enthusiastically welcoming the attention.

The Euclid Avenue Opera House created the synergy for development of retail stores, first-rate restaurants, bars, and the Krause Costume Company, nationally famous for providing superb theatrical outfits. Prominent stage stars visited Jimmy McGlade's Fourth Street restaurant. Café Windsor, opening in 1876, combined an ice cream parlor with sales of Whitman's candies, flowers, and imported and domestic cigars. The Opera House Café and Billiard Parlor advertised the best liquors, cool lager beers, and Havana cigars. A tavern across the street promoted Schlitz's Atlas Beer on draught and good, warm lunches all day. Otto

Moser's and the Rathskeller, two legendary Fourth Street restaurants, opened during this period.

Less revered competitors to the Opera House also emerged. In 1884, the White Elephant Variety Theater, located on Fourth Street between Huron Road and Eagle Avenue, promoted itself as "the finest place of amusement in the west," with amenities including the theater, a bar, eight bowling alleys, a shooting gallery, an ample selection of billiard tables, and a piano player who always wore a striped shirt. The theater grounded the first two floors of the five-story building, with dressing rooms on the upper three floors. The White Elephant's sporadic bookings through 1886 included vaudeville shows, a parlor circus, sacred concerts, Lizzie Webber's burlesque troupe, and wrestling matches with $50 "winner take all" purses. "Percentage girls" received a cut from money paid for the drinks they hustled. In less than two years, the Grand Central Theater replaced the White Elephant, promising "the best artists in the vaudeville profession." Not many artists actually appeared there, and the few that did failed to inspire audiences to place them in even the middle ranks of performers, let alone among the best. A men's social club replaced the theater, surviving until the beginning of Prohibition.

The Central and Sheriff Street markets, both bordering Fourth Street near its southern terminus at Eagle Avenue, converted their immediate neighborhood into a vibrant commercial district. The markets spawned diverse but complementary businesses, many choosing to locate on Fourth Street.

The National Poultry Supply Company sold incubators and poultry foods to market vendors. G. E. Conkey offered pills, powders, laxatives, and other potions and concoctions to treat 56 different ills encountered by fowls. H. A. Redmond manufactured retail shelving and display merchandise, later expanding to sell and service meat cutters, slicers, scales, coffee grinders, and refrigeration cases and equipment. The Glenville Paper Company manufactured grocery bags and brown butcher paper used in wrapping meats. A meat packing and refrigerated storage facility replaced the old Grand Central Theater, remaining until the building burned to the ground. Quick-service restaurants, shoe-repair establishments, and barbershops catered to employees and customers of the markets as well as the supporting businesses.

OTTO MOSER'S RESTAURANT

Otto F. Moser, born in Canton, moved with his family to Cleveland where he became a bartender. In September 1892, Moser opened a tavern located directly opposite the stage door of the Euclid Avenue Opera House. Actors and musicians hurriedly crossed Fourth Street during intermissions to energize themselves with a quick drink or snack. Middle- and upper-class Opera House patrons used a tunnel beneath Fourth Street to travel from the theater to the tavern's downstairs entrance.

In the 1890s, females did not frequent public bars, so ladies entered a basement-level private club called the Cheese Cellar while men migrated to the upstairs main floor. After an Opera House performance, actors and actresses visited the club, often performing private shows for guests. Cheese Cellar Club alumni include George M. Cohan, John Drew, Anna Held, Lillian Russell, Eddie Foy, Eva Tanguary, Robert Mantell, Lew Docstader, Mme. Ernestine Schumann-Heink, and William Faversham, as well as local politicians, journalists, and members of Cleveland's society.

Moser amassed about 1,200 autographed pictures of celebrities visiting his tavern. In addition to the previously mentioned Cheese Cellar members, Moser's picture collection includes John Barrymore, Lionel Barrymore, Ethel Barrymore, W. C. Fields, Edwin Booth, John Philip Sousa, Ellen Terry, Helen Hayes, Cedric Hardwick, Maurice Evans, Edward Everett Horton, Cornelia Otis Skinner, Fanny Brice, Paul Muni, Gertrude Lawrence, and, quite literally, a thousand more.

Otto Moser's walls also displayed the mounted heads of four deer, a wild bear, and a moose named Bullwinkle, along with a papier-mache eagle and a plastic crow.

In 1949, after three generations, the high, beamed ceiling and old-fashioned light globes still remained in Otto Moser's restaurant. *(Cleveland Public Library, Photographic Collection)*

Two patrons enjoy Otto Moser's hospitality in 1952. A portion of the celebrity picture collection is visible in the background. *(Cleveland State University, Cleveland Press Collection)*

Tradition dictated a bride entering the restaurant on her wedding day must climb on the bar and kiss the moose. Through the years, Bullwinkle received many such demonstrations of affection. The old moose eventually lost his left ear, falling from its position of prominence into a patron's bowl of soup.

Although dinner business deteriorated in the 1920s with the double-barreled whammy of Prohibition and the Opera House closing, a loyal lunch crowd still patronized the tavern, and Moser's famous German potato salad and ham remained staples for Cleveland's hungry diners. The Cheese Cellar reinvented itself as a haven for chess tournaments, but, by the 1960s, served only as a storage area for pickles and beer kegs.

In 1942, Otto Moser died of pneumonia a few months prior to his 75th birthday. He

Woolworth's variety store (currently La Strada Restaurant) and Cort's shoe store (now the Greenhouse Tavern) bounded Otto Moser's restaurant for four decades, including the 1960s, the time of this photograph. Otto Moser's is now the site of the Wonder Bar. *(Cleveland State University, Cleveland Press Collection)*

Max "Slapsie Maxie" Joseph, a veteran of Otto Moser's since 1921, and his cousin Jack Joseph purchased the restaurant in 1952. Max moved the meat-slicing operation to its distinctive position in the front window. Max Joseph, rather than Otto Moser, made corned beef sandwiches an institution at the restaurant. This picture, from 1971, captures Max Joseph just before his retirement. *(Cleveland Public Library, Photographic Collection)*

had operated the Fourth Street restaurant for more than 49 years. About six months after his death, the tavern installed its first cash register. Moser had taken pride in never using the not-so-newfangled invention; bartenders and waiters simply deposited paper money in a drawer while loose change accumulated in a pile on a marble slab behind the bar.

After Moser's death, the Lanahan family purchased the restaurant, selling it to cousins Max and Jack Joseph in 1952. Terrazzo replaced the previous sawdust-covered red brick floor, and the drinking crowd enjoyed a new mahogany bar. But most of the restaurant's decor remained almost frozen in time, reflecting its turn-of-the-century glory days.

Ownership of Otto Moser's changed three times during the 1970s. John Pitt, followed by partners Nels Osbeck and David Butler, briefly owned the restaurant between 1971 and 1977. In 1977, Steve Dimotsis and his father purchased the legendary eatery. Dan Bir became a partner when Steve's father retired in 1989. Steve is now in his fourth decade as proprietor. Only Otto Moser served longer as owner.

Steve Dimotsis, born in Greece, came to the United States before his third birthday. His father worked as a tool-and-die maker, later owning taverns including the Zapher at West 150th Street and Lorain Road. Steve's uncle owned the neighboring Sisters Shoppe on Fourth Street for 30 years.

In the 1980s, a man not recognized by the employees walked into the restaurant during the lunch hour. In conversing with the bartender, the customer revealed he had been a regular patron for many years, but, because of an incident 50 years earlier, had not entered the restaurant in a half century. Moser always wore suspenders, and, on a youthful lark when Moser turned his back, the customer stretched the elastic suspender straps until they snapped. Not at all amused, Moser cast out the culprit, warning him never to return. A half-century later, he worked up enough courage to revisit his former favorite eating place.

Renovation of Playhouse Square's showplaces inspired Steve Dimotsis to relocate Otto Moser's to the theater district. In 1994, the restaurant moved to a 5,200-square-foot location, greatly exceeding the 1,800-square-foot space on Fourth Street. The opening of the Playhouse Square restaurant coincided with St. Patrick's Day. Not to miss the lucrative business, Steve drove to Columbus on St. Patrick's Day to obtain his liquor license; he returned at 2:45 in the afternoon, and, with license in hand, opened the bar to thirsty revelers. The celebrity pictures and animal heads still reside on the restaurant's walls, although the deteriorated eagle and crow failed to withstand the move to Playhouse Square.

THE RATHSKELLER

The Rathskeller debuted across from the Euclid Avenue Opera House on October 6, 1900. Henry Grebe owned the restaurant in its hey-day, the first two decades of the 20th Century. In 1920, Grebe paid rent of $15,000 per year to house his booming restaurant. Though crippled by Prohibition, the restaurant remained in business, serving lunches. Favorite menu items consisted of blue points, baby lobster, and cheesecake.

Otto Gross, a former Rathskeller bartender, later owned the restaurant, scaling down its size and catering to workingmen interested primarily in a shot-and-a-beer rather than expensive martinis or cocktails. In 2000, forced with an option to transform the tavern into an upscale bar to offset a substantial rent increase, the Rathskeller moved to Prospect Avenue where it continued as a workingperson's bar. Maintaining a long tradition, Rathskeller regulars still enjoyed beer served in "frosted" glasses that remained refrigerated until requested by a customer. After 110 years, the Rathskeller closed in 2010.

The Rathskeller Restaurant, in its heyday around 1910, seated 600 persons, exclusive of a quick-lunch counter. *(Alan Dutka collection)*

Marjorie Moore and her Melody Maids, one of the all-girl orchestras popular in the 1920s, provided entertainment at Fourth Street's Rathskeller. *(Alan Dutka collection)*

Fourth Street's Maturity as a Retail Center (1900 – 1950)

Property owners converted once-fashionable homes into rooming houses and small hotels, eventually razing the structures for commercial interests. In the 1890s, John C. Lowe remodeled a bicycle shop (current House of Blues Restaurant site) into a manufacturing operation for umbrellas, parasols, and canes. In addition to selling his newly manufactured merchandise, Lowe replaced torn umbrella covers, charging from 35 cents to $1.75. The more expensive replacement covers carried a two-year warranty. In 1902, 27-seven-year-old Mortimer F. Mason began selling men's hats at the new Danbury Hat Store, located in part of the present Lola restaurant site. All hats sold for $2.00. Five years later, he moved across the street to the later McCrory Building site. After eight years at that location, Mason sold his hat shop to pursue a career as an insurance salesman; prospering in his new livelihood, Mason continued selling insurance until his retirement in 1963 at the age of 88. Mason died six years later.

Fourth Street's retail stores failed to attain the high-class prominence reached by some of their downtown neighbors. In 1922, the Newark Shoe Store advertised ladies' plain or strap pumps ($1.95), gun metal lace Oxfords ($2.95), patent leather pumps ($2.95), and black satin pumps ($3.45); in contrast, Linder-Coy's shoes, priced at $8.75, included gore and strap pumps, light brown suede, gray suede, patent, black satin, black kid, and white kid. Next to Newark's Shoes, Sebastian The Hatter priced men's hats in the $3.00 to $5.00 range; at the same time, Euclid Avenue's B. R. Baker charged $7.00, and Hill & Hart, in the Leader Building, commanded $5.00 to $8.00 for each hat. In 1931, the Fourth Street's Cort shoe store advertised hundred of pairs of women's shoes and pumps, in high and low heels, for 97 cents each; Euclid Avenue merchants

The northeast corner of Fourth Street and Prospect Avenue housed Sol Bergman's jewelry company prior to construction of the Sincere Building. Bergman relocated to East Ninth Street, but returned to the identical Fourth Street corner upon completion of the Sincere Building. The jewelry store developed into the largest pawnshop in the state of Ohio. Unredeemed merchandise sold at bargain, although not necessarily inexpensive, prices. *(Ralph Horner)*

charged between $5.00 and $8.00 for a pair of women's shoes.

Although Fourth Street's retail merchandise did not rival its high-end competitors, the crowded stores never lacked shoppers. In 1936, in the midst of the Great Depression, very few business sites stood vacant. The diminutive street, extending from Euclid Avenue to Ontario Street, supported three national variety stores, 12 restaurants, a tavern, five barbers, a men's clothing shop, five shoe stores, two retail jewelry establishments, three hat shops, a paint store, a wallpaper business, two cigar stores, two shoe-repair facilities, a beauty shop, two furniture businesses, a tire-repair outlet, two small hotels, an office supply business, a florist, a grocery store, the Central Market, and the last lingering remnants of the Sheriff Street Market. The street also housed a gospel worker's mission, at least six wholesale meat companies, a restaurant supply business, a butcher supply enterprise, and manufacturers of table mats and wholesale paper. Enormous delivery trucks cluttered Fourth Street while drivers unloaded crates, boxes, and barrels to restock supplies at the three large dime stores. The trucks seemed almost to scrape the buildings as they maneuvered along the narrow street.

EARLY 20TH CENTURY CRIME

In 1918, Harry L. Davis, Cleveland's mayor, cautioned that increases in the boldness of criminals resulted in monetary and property losses in Cleveland of $442,832.38 during 1917. Incidents on Fourth Street mirrored Cleveland's growing crime problem during the First World War and 1920s. In 1918, two bandits fled with a canvas bag containing $2,300 in cash and $2,800 in checks after a daring broad daylight holdup of a Cottage Creamery cashier on his way to deposit the day's receipts at a nearby bank. After subduing their victim by throwing cayenne pepper in his face, the pistol-waving robbers fled to safety in an automobile waiting at the intersection of Fourth Street and Eagle Avenue where the robbery occurred.

Even the rich and famous lacked immunity from the criminal element. In 1919, Mrs. F. A. Seiberling, wife of Goodyear Tire and Rubber founder Frank Seiberling, journeyed with her mother from their palatial Stan Hywet mansion in Akron to attend a Philadelphia Orchestra concert at Grays Armory. The chauffeur guarded a $550 fur coat, picked up after receiving alterations in downtown Cleveland, until he left the automobile unattended to purchase his dinner. Two 18-year-olds vandalized the car, stealing not only the expensive coat but also a suitcase containing the chauffeur's clothes. Police apprehended the youths on Fourth Street near Huron Road, a few blocks from the concert site. Not even Clevelanders, these amateur thieves resided in Toledo and Leetonia.

In 1921, Herbert H. Stoner's restaurant (current site of the Greenhouse Tavern) endured five attempted robberies in a two-month period. Four successful break-ins netted a total of $630 in cash, $600 in jewelry, an overcoat, and a pistol. Thieves in one of the robberies overlooked $400 in a locked safe with the combination clearly displayed in plain sight. The fifth attempt failed when robbers entered the restaurant during business hours, only to encounter two police officers who fired several shots at the fleeing criminals while the lawmen finished their lunch.

Payroll robberies, in vogue in the 1920s, included a 1921 holdup of the Bloch Company, located at the intersection of Fourth Street and Prospect Avenue. Three gunmen escaped with $1,675 as employees transferred the money from the Fourth Street headquarters to a factory on East 55th Street. The robbers crowded the automobile carrying the payroll to the curb. As the fenders of the two cars collided, a gunman standing on the running board of the robber car fell between the two vehicles. He regained his footing and, with revolver in hand, leaped to the running board of the payroll car. A concerned witness viewing the incident concluded the drawn gun merely reflected an argument about the fender-bender; he called the police, reporting someone may have been hurt in an accident, but failed to mention the revolver.

Fourth Street restaurants, mostly south of Prospect Avenue, received numerous citations for producing and selling alcoholic beverages during Prohibition. A grand jury even indicted one Fourth Street merchant for selling the materials required to brew illegal beer.

THE KRAUSE COSTUME SHOP

German orchestras, bands, and singing societies contributed greatly to Cleveland's impressive cultural growth during the second half of the 19th Century. The city hosted five North American Saengerfests between 1855 and 1927, focusing on concerts, dinners, picnics, parades, and balls. In 1858, the Cleveland Gesangverein, another German cultural organization, began producing operas using local talent. The group occupied the building on East 55th Street later used for decades by the House of Wills funeral home.

In 1867, this lively German cultural environment attracted immigrants William Krause and his wife, both actors desiring to perform in America's German theater. The husband-and-wife team created costumes used by Cleveland's German Society. The couple then founded a costume shop on West 6th Street across from the Academy of Music, at the time Cleveland's most prestigious theater. In 1883, Krause moved the business to Fourth Street, directly opposite the thriving Opera House. Charles Krause, a professional tailor, joined his parents' business in 1890, living on Fourth Street above the shop. He became owner when his mother and father retired in 1894.

In 1912, Charles constructed a new building on the same Fourth Street site; Otto Moser's restaurant occupied the street level, with the Krause Costume Shop on the second floor and its tailoring operations above the shop. The sidewalk directly in front of the building must have gained

Portions of the Krause Costume Shop resembled a museum rather than a retail store. This 1969 photograph captures a display at the Superior Avenue location. (Cleveland State University, Cleveland Press Collection)

a somewhat daunting reputation. Prior to the 1912 construction, an affluent but obstinate matron lived in a brownstone above street-level businesses. An eminent lawyer, attempting to visit the headstrong lady, found himself flying down the steps, three at a time, with an airborne lamp in close pursuit. Shortly after construction of the Krause Building, a young man, dressed in full armor and headed for a masquerade party, purchased a false mustache to accent his iron suit. Losing his balance at the top of the stairs, the make-believe knight plunged backwards down the steps, crashed through the street door, and landed on the sidewalk in nearly the same spot where the lawyer had set down earlier.

In 1922, after the Opera House closed, Krause Costumes moved to 1029 Chester Avenue. David Yost, who joined the company in 1918, became owner in 1923. A trained opera singer, Yost had previously toured with opera companies and Broadway and vaudeville stars, including DeWolf Hopper. In the same year he acquired the company,

Yost organized the National Costumers Association, an organization still in existence, now headquartered in Indianapolis.

Krause's customer base included theaters, civic groups, churches, ethnic celebrations, historical pageants, masquerade balls, costume parties, businesses, nightclubs, the general public and, in later years, television studios. Krause rented or sold a huge variety of costumes and accessories, furnishing orders locally and throughout the country. The company could equip an entire cast for *Hamlet* or *Macbeth* with costumes and props, many salvaged during the Opera House demolition. Even into the 1930s, Krause shipped orders to customers in 20 states, including a pair of Santa Claus suits dispatched to Nome, Alaska. Company tailors also manufactured custom-made orders, such as 24 totem-pole outfits critical to a production of *Rose Marie*.

Mustaches, noses, ears, eyebrows, and teeth represented more commonplace requests. Santa Claus suits, complete with wigs, beards, and masks, remained popular for decades. Other timeless attire featured outfits portraying Cleopatra, Napoleon, Southern belles, and the New York Yankees. Trendy costumes included grizzly bear and flapper outfits in the 1920s, zoot suits in the 1940s, Davy Crockett and calypso attire in the 1950s, go-go dancer costumes in the 1960s, and hot pants and disco outfits in the 1970s. Elvis Presley and Halloween apparel rose in popularity in the 1980s.

The company filled glass showcases with genuine German, Austrian, and Hungarian uniforms, Civil War outfits, American marines' attire during the Spanish Civil War, armor, jewels, and other treasures acquired throughout the world. One of Krause's prized possessions, the actual clothing worn by Chief Little Crow when he met his death, contained the hole created by a deadly

bullet fired from a bounty hunter's gun. The garment is a remarkable achievement in historic preservation considering, after the Dakota Sioux chief's death on July 3, 1863, the townspeople of Hutchinson, Minnesota, dragged his mutilated body through the streets. After the vicious celebration, Chief Little Crow's body lay in an alley commonly used to accumulate garbage.

Mel Gerseny purchased the company following David Yost's retirement in 1952. Krause Costumes remained on Chester Avenue until 1967 when construction of the current Ohio Savings headquarters required razing the old building. The costume shop relocated to Superior Avenue, near East 24th Street, where it continued until the company closed in 1985.

In 1945, the Victory Store on Fourth Street near Huron Road, an Army and Navy surplus outlet, offered a Navy double-deck bed in dark walnut for $18.95; the advertising noted, "Sure the wood frames are scratched, but there are years of wear still in them." Other bargains included Army folding cots ($6.95), G. I. raincoats ($7.95), all-purpose Army soap (three pounds for 98 cents), hunting knives

($4.95 to $7.50) and Army officers' pup tents ($10.95). The Royal Shoe Company operated two Fourth Street stores nearly across from each other, one in the Graves Building (now Zocalo Mexican Grill & Tequileria) and one in the Cort Building (now the Greenhouse Tavern). Bargains included children's two-snap galoshes ($1.51) and bunny slippers in pink or blue (94 cents).

THE FREDERICK BUILDING

Throughout most of its history, the white terra cotta Frederick Building, constructed in 1912, supported three street-level retail stores along its 62-foot frontage. The left-most storefront, originally a Krohngold Shoe Store, later became the first location of the Sisters Shoppe. In the 1950s and 1960s, a Farmer's Pride Poultry Store occupied the site. In 1950, the store offered eggs for 54 cents/dozen, chicken legs and breasts at 85 cents/pound, gizzards for 45 cents/pound, and fryers or

roasters for 65 cents/pound. After the poultry store's closing, tenants included a shoe repair and Leeds Imports. TNT Men's Fashions sold clothing in the space for 30 years from 1978 to 2007. This is currently the site of the Erie Island Coffee Shop.

The Normandie Hat Shop operated for nearly 40 years before being replaced in 1974 by Rose Wigs, which remained until 2002. The Sisters Shoppe, specializing in infant's and children's wear, moved from

In 1950, the Frederick Building housed Farmers Pride Poultry Store, the Normandie Hat Shop and Sisters Shoppe. The McCory Variety Store is to the left. *(Cleveland Public Library, Photographic Collection)*

the poultry store location in 1950. In that year, Sisters sold children's car coats, with quilted lining and matching hood, in sizes 1 to 14, for $4.00. Prior to Sisters, a wallpaper company and Sherman Wash and Wear clothing store occupied the site. The Normandie and Sisters locations currently house the Saigon Restaurant.

During the 1950s, a dentist, chiropodist, photographer, and lawyer occupied the second floor. The third floor housed a violin maker, a manufacturer's agent, a beauty shop, an advertising agency, and an architect. A finance company and a construction company's office anchored the fourth floor. The top floor housed a jeweler, a tailor, and typewriter supply company. A picture framer occupied the basement, and the main floor housed a barber. In later years, the upper floors became home to a variety of organizations including Alcoholics Anonymous, the Brotherhood of Railroad Trainmen, the Cleveland Audubon Society, and the Grand Jury Association.

2230 EAST FOURTH STREET: JAZZ LEGENDS AND BELLY DANCERS (1954 – 1979)

A small, unassuming one-story building, situated on Fourth Street between Huron and Bolivar roads, played host to a succession of jazz legends, belly dancers, and stand-up comics during a 37-year stretch between 1954 and 1990.

Prior to this diverse collection of entertainment offerings, the site had already obtained a reputation as one of Fourth Street's early-20th Century hotspots. The Feichtmeier family operated a restaurant a few doors away from 1910 to 1917. In 1918, the family began a 24-year-operation of the Feichtmeier Restaurant at 2230 East Fourth Street. When the restaurant closed in 1942, the Daisy Café occupied the space for less

than one year. A business lunch, consisting of soup and beer, cost 25 cents. A poultry store, the Dredgers Club, the Viking Steak House & Lounge Bar, and the FAB Beer Parlor failed to make a lasting impression on the Fourth Street landscape.

The parade of jazz celebrities began in 1954 with the opening of the Cotton Club, renamed the Modern Jazz Room in 1957. Jim Bard, a psychologist and instructor at Fenn College, teamed with drummer Fats Heard to purchase the club. Heard, a graduate of Cleveland's Central High School and a student at the Cleveland Institute of Music, previously toured with Lionel Hampton and Erroll Garner and achieved legendary status as the featured drummer on Garner's classic recording of "Misty."

The ambience, charitably described as a mixture of dingy and tacky, consisted of chrome and plastic chairs accompanied by tables large enough to hold four cocktail glasses, and not much else. Although lacking in elegant décor, the Modern Jazz Room booked jazz legends Count Basie, Duke Ellington, Dizzy Gillespie, Ella Fitzgerald, Billie Holiday, Sarah Vaughn, Lionel Hampton, Erroll Garner, Buddy Rich, Dave Brubeck, and many others. As performers' pay escalated, the small club could no longer turn a profit booking first-class national artists. After a year as the Down Beat Club, the venue closed in 1961. The site then hosted the Persian Lounge for a very brief period before the arrival of belly dancers.

In 1950, George Koropoulis immigrated

to the United States from Greece. Trained as a chef in Italy, he worked as a busboy at Hotel Cleveland, eventually obtaining a position as a chef. In 1963, Koropoulis opened his innovative Grecian Gardens Restaurant, offering both Grecian and American cuisine. Although popular as a lunch venue, the restaurant is most remembered for the authentic Grecian artists performing at a dinner show (8:30 p.m.) and two supper shows (11:30 p.m. and 1:00 a.m.). Greek vocalists and musicians charmed audiences. Advertisements touted Beba Kyriakidou ("the atomic bomb of the Greek entertainment world") as arriving direct from Athens. The singer and actress had previously performed in the Greek films *Dollars and Dreams* and *Good Times, Money and Love*. But exotic belly dancers quickly became the signature portion of the restaurant's entertainment offerings. Patrons of Greek descent, including actor Telly Savalas, sometimes participated in an exuberant Greek folk dance that culminated in smashing dinner plates onto the floor. Koropoulis owned or co-owned 12 Cleveland restaurants including the nearby Grecian Nites and Never On Sunday venues, both on Bolivar Street. The Grecian Gardens ended its Fourth Street run in 1979.

2230 EAST FOURTH STREET:
THE CLEVELAND COMEDY CLUB
(1980 – 1990)

The Cleveland Comedy Club took over the Grecian Gardens space and served as a launching pad to jumpstart the careers of future film stars, television performers, writers and producers, comedy club entertainers, a Grammy and Emmy awards host, performers playing Radio City and off-Broadway, a booking agent, and a college professor. A large portion of this talent originated in Northeast Ohio high schools.

Drew Carey (James Ford Rhodes High School) won a $50 amateur prize in January 1986. Three months later Carey earned $100 per week as the club's paid emcee. Rick Cleveland (real name Rick Scheiman) (Parma High School) won Emmy and Writers Guild awards for his script contributions to *The West Wing* television program. He also wrote scripts for HBO's *Six Feet Under* and *Gary Unmarried*, and appeared with Chicago's Second City Company.

Steve Harvey (Glenville High School) hosted television's *It's Showtime at the Apollo* and starred in other programs, including *The Steve Harvey Show* and *The Steve Harvey Morning Show*. Special K. McCray, (JFK High School) appeared in films, including *China Moon* and *Rush*. Jimmy Malone (Shaker Heights High School) developed a *Knuckleheads in the News* routine highlighting stories of ordinary people doing stupid things. He became a partner with John Lanigan on the popular *Lanigan & Malone* radio show.

Steve Skrovan (Gilmour Academy), a Yale graduate, served as an executive producer and writer for the television show *Everybody Loves Raymond* and wrote material for the *Seinfeld* show. John Henton (Shaw High School), a student of computer science at Cuyahoga Community College and Ohio State, performed on television's *Living Single* and *The Hughleys*. Bob Palmer (Midpark High School) worked on the Lanigan & Webster radio show and toured comedy club circuits.

Audiences booed North Ridgeville's Jeff Shaw off the Comedy Club stage just

three minutes into his monologue. From that humble beginning, Shaw has performed more than 5,000 comedy routines in comedy clubs, colleges, universities, casinos, and cruise lines. Seth Isler, a Cleveland Heights native, performed on *The Drew Carey Show*, *NYPD Blue*, and *Friends*, and he also developed *The Godfaddah Workout*, a one-man off-Broadway show in which he plays all the major characters in the *Godfather* film. Wickliffe's Terry Mulroy has written for *The Drew Carey Show* and written and co-produced the television shows *Still Standing* and *According to Jim*. Lakewood native Carol Pennington performed in comedy clubs and colleges and universities from Alaska to Florida. She owns Hysterical Management, a nationally known comedy booking agency located in Macedonia.

The Comedy Club helped launch the careers of three Collinwood natives: A. J. Jamal, Carmen Ciricillo, and Hector Rezzano. Jamal, a former *Plain Dealer* carrier and graduate of Kent State University, began a business career as an IBM engineer. His fellow workers at IBM raised $10,000 as seed money to launch his comedy career. Jamal appeared on *The Tonight Show* with Jay Leno, HBO's *Comic Relief*, and the long-running *In Living Color*. He has appeared in diverse venues including Radio City and Caesar's Palace. Carmen Ciricillo, known as the Construction Comic for his routines depicting the life of a contractor, has opened for Englebert Humperdinck and Michael Bolton, and has successfully toured for 20 years. Hector Rezzano began his career on one of the club's amateur nights, successfully toured the national nightclub circuit, but tragically succumbed to leukemia.

Comedy Club alumnus Mike Geither earned a degree in literature and creative writing from Cleveland State University and an MFA in playwriting from the University of Iowa. He is currently an Assistant Professor at Cleveland State University. Herb Petrait, a Cleveland businessman, sold his American Academy of Driving business to concentrate on comedy. Sadly, Petrait died in the 1990s.

The Comedy Club also provided early exposure for many entertainers not associated with Cleveland. La Vance Lining, now a successful standup Christian comic, won the Comedy Club's Amateur Night competition eight consecutive times. Garry Shandling wrote scripts for *Sanford And Son*, *Three's Company*, and *Welcome Back Kotter*; he guest-hosted Johnny Carson's

Tonight Show, and hosted both Grammy and Emmy award programs He used the Comedy Club to sharpen his standup routines after deciding to switch from writing to performing. Tom Anderson wrote scripts for *Living Single*, created the *Jeff Foxworthy Show*, and produced the final season of *Cheers*. Dom Irrera earned five American Comedy Awards nominations for Best Male Standup. He appeared on many television talk shows and sitcoms.

The Cleveland Comedy Club enjoyed an 11-year run until succumbing to the Gateway sports construction in 1990.

GIGI'S RESTAURANT

Gigi's Montmartre de Cleveland graced Fourth Street for nearly a quarter century between 1960 and 1983. A unique blend of experience, creativity, and customer relations combined to generate the restaurant's reputation for excellence. Beginning at the age of 10, Irma Rassie, the wife of George Rassie, the restaurant's Lebanese owner, learned her cooking skills from an Austrian-German grandmother. Gigi's menu, designed by a French chef lured from New York's Waldorf-Astoria, included chef salad Julienne, broiled Mediterranean shrimp, frog legs, lobster thermidor, stuffed boneless chicken breast, and chateaubriand. A popular molded dessert combined grasshopper crème de menthe, crème de cacao, and whipped cream. But dessert connoisseurs treasured Cherries Jubilee, the restaurant's supreme after-dinner indulgence. At tableside, a server ignited a pan of cherries combined with Kirschwasser liqueur, pouring the flaming treat over ice cream. The almost shamefully extravagant delight, designed to be shared by a couple, cost an outrageous $4.50.

George Rassie sometimes enforced the restaurant's dress code with uncommon zeal.

Gigi's Restaurant, a popular Fourth Street eating establishment in the 1960s and 1970s, is now a Harry Buffalo Restaurant. *(Alan Dutka collection)*

Noticing an otherwise well-healed patron wearing a coat with a conspicuously ragged inner lining, Rassie sent the garment to be mended while the unsuspecting customer enjoyed lunch. In another instance, Rassie observed a patron's necktie which he considered unbecoming. He clipped off the offending necktie, giving the surprised dinner customer enough money to purchase a more attractive tie.

Gigi's site had been a saloon or restaurant since the turn of the century, its dining and drinking history interrupted for only five years in the 1930s by a women's clothing store, an incandescent lamp dealer, and a men's hat shop. In the 1950s, Rassie operated a restaurant, unimaginatively named the George Rassie Restaurant, at the same location; he later renamed it Roxy's Café. After Gigi's, the site housed the Apres Vous Café, the Star Bar and Grill, and the Ferris Steakhouse. A Harry Buffalo restaurant currently resides in the only remaining Fourth Street building still standing south of Prospect Avenue.

Decades of Decline (1950 – 1995)

Beginning in the 1950s, Fourth Street declined steadily, a consequence of retail's unrelenting shift to the suburbs. Retail at the Windsor Block evolved from a dry goods store to, in succession, Wig Land, U. S. Hair, and Lee's Beauty Supply. The Cort Building, noted for its shoe stores, became the American Wig Company and U. S. Hair (Greenhouse Tavern site). The Krause Building, once the home of Otto Moser's Restaurant, housed Fast Cash (Wonder Bar site). The Buckeye Building transformed its retail space from a restaurant to a check cashing facility (Flannery's Pub site). Kresge's variety store became U. S. Hair and Star Beauty (Pickwick & Frolic site). Retail at the Frederick Building changed from the Normandie Hat Shop to Rose Wigs (Saigon Restaurant site). The Graves Building, once home to a shoe store, turned into a pawn shop (Zocalo Mexican Grill & Tequileria site).

Mother Olga, a Fourth Street veteran since the 1950s, expanded her Gold Teacup fortune-telling room into the Miracle Faith Tabernacle, operating daily from 9:00 a.m. to 6:00 p.m. in a former barbershop located just south of Gigi's Restaurant. In the 1960s, Olga, the resident healer and advisor, charged $2.00 for readings and, for an additional fee, promised to "remove unnatural sickness from your body, call your enemies by name, and tell you who to keep away from, and show you how to remove pain and all bad luck." Advertised testimonials from past clients praised Olga's extraordinary abilities:

"I was flat on my back suffering from an incurable disease. There was no hope until I heard of and saw Mrs. Olga. Thank God for her; I am well."

"I have had bad luck and been under evil influences for many years. I could not hold a job until I heard of and saw Mrs. Olga, and I have a steady job now and I am feeling fine."

In 1971, newspaper columnist George Condon commented, "East Fourth Street has deteriorated into a seedy side street." But in the early 1980s, the street still teemed with activity. Merchants piled fashion bargains on outside tables as enthusiastic shoppers, searching for spectacular deals, blocked the narrow sidewalks in front of Rainbow Jewelry, Modern Menswear, TNT Men's Fashions, Fashion Express, Lynn's Apparel, and Sisters Shoppe.

A formidable street gang rumble, resulting in looting and vandalism, rocked Fourth Street in the early morning hours of Sunday, February 5, 1981. A mammoth brawl, involving between 200 and 300 members of four Cleveland gangs, erupted at the Giant Juke Box, a disco located at 1910 Euclid Avenue. One of the disco lovers departed the uproar, only to return with a loaded shotgun. The Giant Juke Box prematurely closed, sending many underage patrons on a pre-sunrise stroll down Euclid Avenue to Public Square, apparently in search of buses since the 15- and 16-year-olds lacked easy access to automobiles. As the crowd neared Public Square, rioting broke out, resulting in the looting of U.S. Hair, Royal Shoes, Han's International Corporation, Woolworth's variety store, Modern Menswear, the All State Beauty Supply Company, and Sisser Jewelers. Thirty police officers labored for 45 minutes to quell the disturbance. The gangs then proceeded to Public Square, creating additional commotion as they impatiently awaited their buses. The Regional Transit Authority cooperated by dispatching extra vehicles to help disperse the looters and rioters.

In summer 1976, Fourth Street closed to automobile traffic for two months as merchants promoted "the Fourth Street mall." In this photograph, entertainment is provided by the DeJarnette Jazz Company with Lamarr Baker on drums. *(Cleveland State University, Cleveland Press Collection)*

The striking contrast between the recently opened 200 Public Square Building (BP Building) and Fourth Street's Krause Building is captured on November 6, 1988. *(City of Cleveland, Landmarks Commission, Donn R. Nottage)*

In 1956, Morlins Gift Shop replaced a Fanny Farmer candy store in the Windsor Block facing Euclid Avenue. Thirty years later, Morlins moved to the Frederick Building where it remained until 1993. The store, resembling an imported goods bazaar, carried merchandise ranging from dish towels, whisk brooms, and low-priced transistor radios to expensive capodimonte table pieces. This picture is from December 30, 1988. *(City of Cleveland, Landmarks Commission, Warner Thomas)*

The west side of Fourth Street, looking south to Prospect Avenue, has changed dramatically with fashionable restaurants replacing shoe stores, wig shops, and bar/restaurant combinations. Just out of the range of this 1976 photograph is Wig Land (House of Blues Restaurant). Proceeding south are Royal Shoes and the American Wig Company (Greenhouse Tavern), Otto Mosher's (Wonder Bar), the Rathskeller (La Strada Restaurant), Downtown Fabrics and the J&G Shoe Box (Lola Restaurant) and All Star Beauty Supply and Sisser Jewelry (Flannery's Irish Pub). The Kurtz Furniture site, now a parking lot, is on the corner of Fourth Street and Prospect Avenue. *(Cleveland State University, Cleveland* Press *Collection)*

Rainbow Jewelry occupied this site from 1983 to 1997, although the location is mostly associated with shoe stores; Chisholm Shoes opened in 1906, and Cort Shoes operated for nearly four decades in this store between 1931 and 1973. The Greenhouse Tavern is the current tenant. This photograph is from 1995. *(Cleveland Public Library, Photographic Collection)*

THE SINCERE BUILDING

Through the years, the Sincere Building, built in 1898, has been the headquarters for the Cuyahoga County Socialist Party, a barber's union, and a publisher of a Jewish newspaper. Tenants have included manufacturers of violins, washing machines, cutlery, and jewelry. It also housed a detective agency; repair service for clocks, watches, cameras, handbags, and shoes, beauty supply companies; doctors; dentists; attorneys; insurance agents; accountants; printers; jewelers; tailors; artists; architects; barbers, and photographers. The Boy Scouts once used the entire sixth floor as a headquarters, including an information bureau and council room equipped with a large open fireplace and grill.

In 1965, Napoleon Mason's Mortgage and Real Estate Company, a respected business, offered to pay eight percent interest on investments of as low as $2.00 per week. The Modern Business School prepared students for Civil Service examinations. Factory Outlet Wigs celebrated its grand opening on December 26, 1970, remaining in the building through 1983. The company priced wash-and-wear stretch wigs, in dynel and modacrylic synthetic fibers, from $5.95.

An October 5, 1974, advertisement in the *Call & Post* suggested readers send $1.00 with a self-addressed, stamped envelope to 2077 East Fourth Street (Sincere Building address) to obtain a special blessing. A free-will donation could be given after the reader experienced success. The advertisement noted this offer actually exceeded a money-back guarantee.

In 1980, the Sincere Building closed all floors above the street level. Nick Zarnes purchased the building in 2001. On the day he took possession, the proud new owner drove downtown to inspect his new acquisition, only to discover the doors had been boarded up by the City of Cleveland. One of the few remaining tenants faced arrest for selling drugs in the building's basement. Zarnes evicted a group of fortune-telling gypsies who had not paid rent in three years. Later allowing a competing gypsy to practice her fortune-telling trade on the Prospect side of the building, Zarnes unknowingly became involved in a territorial war among the gypsies that required use of his mediation skills.

THE FIRST WOOLWORTH STORE BUILDING

From 1916 to 1950, the F. W. Woolworth Company used this site as a side entrance to its first Euclid Avenue store.

In 1966, the short-lived Discount Book Store offered a set of four books with the intriguing titles *She Strips You, She Whips You, She Binds You,* and *She Defeats You,* each volume selling for the bargain price of $2.50. These books, along with many similar offerings, appealed primarily to businessmen shopping during lunch hour. The Discount Book Store is sometimes confused with the later and more successful Fourth Street Book Exchange, located at the intersection of Fourth and High streets, and especially noted for an extensive selection of pornographic material. The Book Exchange site is now a surface parking lot charging $35 for special sports events at the Quicken Loans Arena.

This building housed the American Mills

The Discount Book Store, operating in 1966, failed to initiate a cultural revolution among Fourth Street's shoppers. *(Cleveland State University, Cleveland* Press *Collection)*

Dry Goods Company in the early 1960s; in 1963, bargains included Cannon wash towels (nine cents), nylon hosiery (29 cents) and boys' T-shirts (four for $1.00). La Mar's Hoffman House Restaurant, Ivy's Pub, the Music Grotto, Wig Land, U. S. Hair, and Lee's Beauty Supply followed the book store as tenants. This is the current site of the House of Blues Restaurant.

NEW YORK COMPARISONS

Fourth Street has often invoked comparisons with New York City. In 1973, the *Call & Post* believed the intersection of Fourth Street and Prospect Avenue captured the ambiance of Harlem's 125th Street and Lenox Avenue (also known as Malcolm X Boulevard) because of its predominantly black shopping area. In the 1990s, the *Plain Dealer* characterized Fourth Street as emitting a "honky-tonk appearance reminiscent of sections of New York's lower east side." In the 21st Century, a nearby restaurant owner recalled memories of Fourth Street as a dull alley filled with uninspiring stores. With maturity, he now visualizes the scene from his youth as a potential setting for a Damon Runyon story.

Alan Glazen, owner of the Erie Island Coffee Shop, sees a present similarity to New York because Fourth Street is packed with independent competing businesses. To succeed, each business must deliver excellence in its own way.

Ari Maron, whose company owns and developed the block, views Fourth Street strictly in terms of Cleveland. Maron observes, unlike New York City, nearly everyone he meets reminiscences about once shopping or working on the old street, or, in some cases, even deliberately avoiding it. Whatever the comparison, Fourth Street exudes an elusive "character" found woefully missing in sterile suburban shopping centers.

For at least the past 40 years, Fourth Street has drawn comparisons to streets located in New York City. This photograph of the narrow street jam-packed with storefronts is late-1980s vintage. *(Historic Gateway Neighborhood Corporation and Bob Zimmer)*

Lynn's clothing shop occupied the former McCrory's variety store site. In this photograph from the mid-1980s, the Vogue Beauty Academy occupies the second floor above Lynn's. Fourth Street stores visible south of Lynn's are TNT Men's Fashions, Rose Wigs, Sisters Shoppe, Morlins, Campus Shoes, and Star Beauty Supply. Just beyond the range of this photograph is Fashion Plus Jewelry. *(City of Cleveland, Landmarks Commission, Warner Thomas)*

THE McCRORY BUILDING

From 1925 to 1955, the McCrory Company occupied a Fourth Street building as a side entrance to its variety store. After McCrory's closed, Lynn's remained a Fourth Street icon for three decades. In 1958, the store sold ladies' leather-like plastic jackets ($6.60); girl's linen-like sailor suits ($2.58); ladies' Sanforized fully lined car coats ($2.99); girl's all-wool coat, hat, and bag sets ($8.98); boy's lined gabardine trench coats ($6.00), and sport jacket and flannel slack combinations ($4.98).

Five years later, customers purchased orlon cardigan sweaters ($1.99), ladies' coats ($17.00), permanently pleated dresses ($1.00), boys' two-piece suits ($7.99), and children's corduroy jumpers ($1.00) and washable slacks ($1.00).

FOURTH STREET'S BEAUTY COLLEGES

After McCrory's variety store closed in 1955, the building's second floor housed three beauty schools: the Ohio Beauty College (1958 - 1966), the American School of Beauty Culture (1968 - 1969), and the Vogue Beauty Academy (1978 - 2004).

In the 1960s, graduates of the Ohio Beauty College completed 1,500 hours of combined theory and hands-on training. Students learned how to cut various hairstyles, dye and straighten hair, and give permanents. Training also included makeup application and skin and nail care. Ambitious high school students and graduates scheduled day and evening classes to accommodate their individual needs. The Fourth Street location offered students the extra benefit of easy encounters with boys attending a barber's college around the corner on Prospect Avenue. In 1965, clients paid $1.75 for haircuts and $3.50 for hairstyling.

Thomas LaMarca founded the Vogue Beauty Academy in the 1950s. His son Marc, an ex-marine, graduated from the school in 1973, becoming owner when Thomas retired. In the 1990s, the academy charged $8,200 tuition for 1,500 hours of instruction, the same amount of time required 40 years earlier. Federal grants constituted the major source of tuition for students, primarily minority women. In 2005, the school charged $35 for a basic men's cornrow, up to $100 for elaborate crazy braids, and about $300 for micro-braids that required five to six hours to design.

In 1995, a student at the Vogue Beauty Academy learns her trade by performing on-the-job training. The landmark Rathskeller Restaurant is across the street; the Woolworth variety store is still in operation to the right.
(Cleveland Public Library, Photographic Collection)

THE GRAVES BUILDING

Built in 1898, the Graves Building, located just north of Prospect Avenue on the east side of Fourth Street, contained four floors. Samuel E. Graves began his career selling groceries, switching to a clerk's job at the forerunner to the May Company. He quickly progressed to a sales position, which he held for 15 years. In 1890, Graves opened his own Euclid Avenue store offering "the highest class of novelties in fine clothing, hats and furnished goods." This business venture failed after four years. Graves toiled for three companies during the next eight years before testing his entrepreneurial ability a second time by opening the S. E. Graves Clothing Company on Fourth Street. He sold "super excellent suits and overcoats" for $10.00 to $15.00 and trousers for $2.50, $3.50, and $4.50. Comparing his Fourth Street location to competitors on Euclid Avenue, Graves described his distinct advantage: "The rent is low although the location is good. Our expenses are trifling." Unfortunately, his sales must have matched the trifling expenses. Graves' second company existed for only three years. After two short sales stints with clothing stores and still not cured of his entrepreneurial desires, Graves opened his own tailoring shop on Wade Park Avenue, later moving to Superior Avenue. The tailor shop remained in business for five years, after which Graves returned to selling.

Later adding two additional floors, the Graves Building has housed restaurants, shoe and jewelry stores, clothing shops, a second-hand cash register company, printers, bookbinders, a picture frame company, jewelry manufacturers, a pawn shop, and a nail care establishment. From 1929 to 1963, Stanley Fell, a dress manufacturing company, occupied floors three though six.

King's Fourth Street Pawnshop, displaying bright red signage, operated in the site now occupied by the Zocalo Mexican Grill & Tequileria. Morlins Gift Shop is to the left. The photograph is from 1995. *(Cleveland Public Library, Photographic Collection)*

The Amazing Renaissance
(1996 – Present)

Fourth Street's remarkable revitalization began with the unleashing of the Gateway sports complex in 1994. In 1990, Cuyahoga County residents narrowly (198,390 to 185,209) approved a cigarette and beer tax that financed its construction. Citizens of Cleveland overwhelmingly defeated the issue while suburban votes accounted for its success. Michael White, Cleveland's mayor, and County Commissioners Tim Hagan, Mary Boyle, and Jim Petro strongly supported the tax while its political opponents included past Cleveland mayor Dennis Kucinich, future Cleveland mayor Frank Jackson, the United Auto Workers, and politicians Louis Stokes and Mary Rose Oakar.

The majority of Fourth Street, south of Prospect Avenue, vanished completely during Gateway construction,

succumbing to sports venues which hosted a pair of World Series contests, an NBA championship, two United States Figure Skating finals, and numerous other events. What remained of the northern portion of the street, between Prospect and Euclid avenues, changed dramatically. By the end of the decade, fashionable loft apartments replaced long-deserted upper floors in the

Fourth Street changed from an old concrete road into an attractive brick street with this renovation completed in 1995. *(Cleveland Public Library, Photographic Collection)*

A decaying Fourth Street, photographed with snow-covered sidewalks in 1997, would soon be transformed into an urban entertainment center. *(Cleveland Public Library, Photographic Collection)*

Henry Berger operated a jewelry store for 45 years (1928-1972) in the building later housing Fashion Plus Jewelry (1975-1995) and Sharon's Psychic Studio (1996-2008).
(Bob Zimmer)

Razing of the building that once housed Sharon's Psychic Studio created an alley now used as an entrance to the Zocalo Mexican Grill and Tequileria.
(James A. Toman)

Buckeye Building and Windsor Block, the south and north anchors of the street's west side. The 21st Century welcomed stylish restaurants, a comedy club doing double-duty as a Sunday morning church, a coffee shop, a 16-lane bowling alley, and a concert stage attracting national acts.

Physical renovations completed in 1995 and 2004 transformed Fourth Street into an aesthetically pleasing, curved, one-lane brick and stone road. Gaslight-style street lamps and attractive 20-foot wide sidewalks encouraged outdoor summer dining. At the other extreme, heated coils, installed beneath the street and sidewalks, mitigated Cleveland's winter snow and slush. In 2006, Fourth Street closed to traffic from May through September, allowing trendy dining tables to expand into the street. Two years later, the street became totally pedestrian-friendly, closing permanently to automobile traffic.

The alluring annual landscaping,

first developed in 2008, is a joint effort of two Cleveland organizations, ParkWorks and the Downtown Cleveland Alliance. ParkWorks designs, plants, inspects and prunes the urban garden while the Downtown Alliance provides the essential daily watering. The 2010 edition included purple and lime coleus, New Guinea impatiens, spider plants, green sedum Angelina, flowering torenia, setcrasewa, purple and green sweet potato vines, mandevilla vines, green fountain grass, and trailing impatiens. In total, the impressive artistic endeavor featured 1,031 plants and flowers displayed in 137 planters and copper sconces. The planters decorated restaurant patios while the sconces adorned walls of buildings. Medical Mutual of Ohio, the City of Cleveland, MRN (the developer of Fourth Street) and local merchants helped defray the $130,000 cost of the impressive landscaping.

The attractive street improvements coincided with Cleveland's growth as a center for cutting-edge dining. Steven Michaelides, a retired former editor of *Restaurant Hospitality*, succeeded in boosting the culinary profile of his home city by conducting a letter-writing campaign inviting influential food critics to Cleveland. Michaelides helped create momentum among the national media to include Cleveland among the cities supporting cutting-edge chefs.

About the same time, writer Michael Ruhlman, another Clevelander, authored *The Making of a Chef*, a book dedicated to the business of professional cooking and its celebrity chefs. Its success spawned two additional books, *The Soul of a Chef* and *The Reach of a Chef*. Ruhlman, no ordinary author, enrolled in the Culinary Institute of America, taking a variety of classes to gain a first-hand understanding of culinary education.

Michael Symon's Lola, the first Fourth Street restaurant worthy of "celebrity chef" status, opened in 2007. *(Positivelycleveland, Jeff Greenberg)*

Cleveland received international publicity when Ruhlman's *The Soul of a Chef* presented an in-depth examination of Lola, Michael Symon's restaurant then located in Tremont. Ruhlman even described the experience of sitting at the same table with renowned food critic John Mariani as he evaluated Lola for an article in *Esquire* magazine. *The New York Times Book Review* called *The Soul of a Chef* "a hold-your-breath-while-you-turn-the-page thriller." In a subsequent article, Mariani acknowledged Michaelides' letter-writing campaign, admitted his guilt in ignoring Cleveland, recognized the city's growth in culinary expertise, and finished the article with the comment, "Now, no more letters." Michaelides and Ruhlman laid initial groundwork for Fourth Street's transformation into a street noted for its celebrity chefs.

The street's revitalization also resulted in the closure or relocation of long-established and profitable businesses. The Rathskeller moved to Prospect Avenue rather than transform itself into an upscale bar. Mrs. Soonja (Sue) Kim, owner of Hair Plus Beauty Supply, relocated from Fourth Street to the Colonial Arcade after she lost her lease, only to experience the same fate at her new location. Her business is now located on St. Clair Avenue near East 76th Street. Other merchants surviving into the 21st Century but no longer remaining on Fourth Street include U. S. Hair, Lee's Beauty Supply, Great Look, Magic Nail, Sisser Jewelers, Alex and Michael Jewelers, Miracle Jewelers, TNT Men's Fashions, Downtown Records & Tapes, and Gamble Flowers and Gifts.

Downtown Cleveland changed dramatically in the second half of the 20th Century. Its once ubiquitous department stores and exclusive shops exist today mostly in fading pictures and dimming recollections of past generations. But Cleveland's current downtown revival, stimulated in part by Fourth Street's emphasis on entertainment and fine dining, is generating new sets of memories created by first dates, marriage proposals, anniversary celebrations, company parties, bowling tournaments, and community service projects sponsored by an urban church. These will be the recollections that future grandparents convey to their offspring as they recall the downtown Cleveland of the early 21st Century.

Fourth Street, no longer open to automobile traffic, is an attractive pedestrian passageway with dramatic landscaping and stylish outdoor seating. In this view looking north, customers are enjoying drinks at La Strada Restaurant; across the street, the Corner Alley is located in the dominant Kresge Building with Pickwick & Frolic directly to the south; the Arcade, on Euclid Avenue, is in the background.
(Positivelycleveland, Scott Meivogel)

Chapter II
Opera House Tales

TIMELINE

1875   John Ellsler launched the Euclid Avenue Opera House after months of construction delays.

1877   Maurice Barrymore became the first of the Barrymore family to perform on the Opera House stage.

1879   Mark Hanna purchased the Opera House at a sheriff's sale.

1884   Hanna hired Augustus Hartz as the Opera House manager.

1886   The Metropolitan Opera Company made its Cleveland debut at the Opera House.

1892   Fire gutted the interior of the Opera House.

1893   The rebuilt Opera House received rave reviews.

1902   The stage version of *Ben-Hur* made the first of seven appearances at the Opera House.

1908   The Opera House hosted the first Cleveland appearance of the *Ziegfeld Follies*.

1913   The Opera House booked its first movie, Sarah Bernhard in *Oedipus Rex*.

1922   The Opera House closed, unable to compete with Playhouse Square's new Hanna and Ohio theaters.

The theatrical excellence of John Ellsler and his daughter Effie elevated Cleveland's reputation as a center for drama in the 19th century.
(Alan Dutka collection)

Bob Hope, Paul Newman, and Tom Hanks are a few of the entertainment superstars who, in the 20th Century, used Cleveland theaters as their initial training ground. Much earlier, John Ellsler reigned as Cleveland's 19th Century star maker, demonstrating superb creative talents as an actor, producer, mentor, and theater owner. Ellsler transformed the Academy of Music, located on West 6th Street, into one of America's most prestigious theaters with a first-rate resident stock company, a well-respected drama school, and performances by the nation's best actors. One well-known performer even entered into in a business partnership with Ellsler to acquire a Pennsylvania oil property. Ellsler incurred a reasonable amount of government scrutiny when his colleague, John Wilkes Booth, assassinated Abraham Lincoln.

The Academy of Music opened on West 6th Street in the Warehouse District on April 16, 1853. John Ellsler transformed the variety theater into one of the country's most celebrated showplaces. In 1889, a fire partially destroyed the theater; three years later, another fire completely gutted the building's interior. Construction of a new Academy Building, which survived until 1974, incorporated the walls of the old theater. The site is currently a parking lot. *(Cleveland Public Library Photographic Collection)*

Following the Civil War, Cleveland's population escalated to about 100,000 residents, with further growth seeming almost inevitable. Nearby smaller towns, including Columbus and Akron, had constructed grand new theaters, leading Ellsler to conclude Cleveland also needed a larger and more elegant playhouse. The opening of the Euclid Avenue Opera House on Fourth Street fulfilled Ellsler's fondest dream, but it then proceeded to ruin the remainder of his life. Along this turbulent path, some of the nation's foremost actors received their early training under Ellsler's affectionate guidance at the Academy of Music and the Opera House.

Ellsler married a fellow thespian, and in the process, gained a seasoned performer for his stock company. Their daughter, Effie, inheriting the acting skills gushing from her parents' genes and taking full advantage of the top-flight dramatic school at her disposal, learned the acting trade quickly. She made her stage debut, at the age of eight, playing Little Eva in a production of *Uncle Tom's Cabin*. Following two decades of performing at

Effie Ellsler, known locally as "Cleveland's sweetheart," followed in her father footsteps as a skilled actor. *(Alan Dutka collection)*

the Academy of Music and the Opera House, Effie converted her first Broadway appearance, playing a young lover in the title role of *Hazel Kirke*, into a magnificent artistic and commercial success. She continued in the coveted role for three years as the show shattered Broadway's previous record for longevity, spawning five simultaneous touring companies. Four decades later, the talented and versatile actress created another Broadway triumph

playing an elderly spinster in *The Bat*.

Between *Hazel Kirke* and *The Bat*, Effie appeared in numerous other Broadway productions and toured extensively. In her 70s, she embarked on a movie career consisting of 22 films, beginning in the silent era and continuing through the

transition to talkies. Even though her days as a leading lady by that time existed only in stage memories, Effie matured into a successful, if type-cast, character actress playing successive roles as an aging woman in a number of productions. At the age of 81, Effie acted in her final film, Greta Garbo's 1936 classic *Camille*. After appearing on the stage or screen nearly her entire life, Effie died six years later.

Clara Morris, another graduate of Ellsler's stock company, migrated to Cleveland from Toronto when her mother discovered she shared her husband with a previously unknown second wife. Beginning at the age of 11, Clara supplemented her mother's paltry housekeeper wages by performing in Ellsler's stock company, initially as a juvenile ballerina. She progressed rapidly into mature acting assignments. After seven somewhat exasperating years with the company, Clara realized Ellsler's wife and daughter had a lock on the choice female roles. She joined a New York stock company and later prospered as an independent actress playing leads in *Camille* and *Jane Eyre*. Clara failed to equal Effie Ellsler's durability as an actress, hampered by poor health, an addiction to morphine, and a declining public interest in her melodramatic style. Discarding her deteriorating acting career, Clara authored books, a newspaper column, and magazine articles until her death as an invalid at the age of 79.

Joe Haworth unsuccessfully applied for an acting position with Ellsler at the age of ten. While Haworth nurtured an early interest in the stage, more practical concerns motivated his youthful job search. His father died in a Confederate prison camp, and the family needed money to support his widowed mother, a younger brother, three sisters, and himself.

Haworth obtained work at a Cleveland newspaper, continuing his relentless pursuit of an acting career. After eight frustrating years, Ellsler finally acquiesced and allowed Haworth to recite an Irish poem during a benefit engagement. Haworth earned a huge audience ovation, rave reviews, and his coveted position in Ellsler's stock company where he subsequently performed in hundreds of productions, many opposite Effie Ellsler.

After four years, Haworth abandoned Cleveland to seek fame and fortune with prestigious touring companies. His blossoming career temporarily climaxed as he unwillingly participated in a bizarre performance, certainly one of the theater's most unusual show-stopping presentations. On tour in Montreal, his leading lady Emily Rigl unexpectedly ended her evening's performance, in the middle of a scene, by announcing Haworth had made her life so unbearable she could no longer continue acting on the same stage with him. Following this tantalizing proclamation, Rigl departed the theater, leaving a

flabbergasted Haworth the unenviable task of adlibbing about possible sources for Emily's frustrations. The strange incident prematurely ended the entire tour. Emily later explained her aggravations by claiming Haworth made passionate love to her, at the same time alerting an advance agent not to include her in future publicity literature.

Haworth's mother died one month after this disastrous road trip, and the stressful period resulted in his suffering a mental breakdown. After a rest in Cleveland, Haworth re-established himself as a formidable actor. In 1903, at age 48, after returning to Cleveland for a summer respite in anticipation of a national fall tour, Haworth unexpectedly succumbed to heart failure.

James O'Neill, a budding Broadway superstar, spent two years with John Ellsler's stock company. He later originated the famous *Count of Monte Cristo* role, performing the part about 6,000 times. During his Ellsler period, in 1877, O'Neill married at least one fair

James O'Neill's *Monte Cristo* epitomized the striking changes in touring show productions. In the 1880s, *Monte Cristo* appeared at the Opera House in repertory with other offerings featuring O'Neill in the lead role. By 1901, the show had been upgraded to a full-fledged extravaganza. Advertisements promoted its large cast, special effects including a spectacular storm scene, and stunning scenery highlighted by a forest at Fontainebleau and the marvelous Hotel Le Moncerf. O'Neill played the lead in seven separate engagements at the Opera House.
(Alan Dutka collection)

maiden from Cleveland. Ella Quinlan, the daughter of a book store owner on Superior Avenue. After their marriage, another Clevelander, Nettie Walsh, sued O'Neill for divorce and child support. James and Nettie had lived together during O'Neill's Cleveland stock company days, and Nettie referred to herself as Mrs. James O'Neill. A judge, although failing to discover enough evidence to substantiate a valid marriage between O'Neill and Walsh, could not be convinced of James' complete purity and ordered O'Neill to pay child support for Nettie's son Alfred. When Alfred reached adulthood and the support checks ended, he sued O'Neill to exonerate his mother's dishonored name. After three years of legal battles, the two reached an out-of-court settlement. Meanwhile, James and Ella produced three legitimate sons, one being the acclaimed playwright Eugene O'Neill.

Not all celebrities rising from Ellsler's

The Euclid Avenue Opera House, Cleveland's most prestigious theater, graced Fourth Street from 1875 to 1922.
(Alan Dutka collection)

EUCLID AVENUE OPERA HOUSE.

organization performed on the stage. One of the most powerful and influential forces in American theatrical history began his career by renting opera glasses and selling candy in the lobby of the Academy of Music. From his merchandise-hawking beginning, Abe Erlanger progressed to treasurer of the Opera House. Straight from his Cleveland duties, Erlanger formed a partnership with Marcus Klaw, creating a theatrical booking agency in New York City with Effie Ellsler among its prestigious clients.

Klaw and Erlanger next organized a large chain of prominent playhouses, joining with leading theater operators and producers to form the Theatrical Syndicate. This organization established systemized booking networks throughout the U.S. encompassing nearly 700 theaters and creating a monopoly over every aspect of contracts and bookings. Similar to John D. Rockefeller's domination of the oil industry, Klaw and Erlanger even owned a costume manufacturing business and an opera company. The two produced dozens of successful Broadway shows; many of these productions, including *Ben-Hur* and *Mr. Blue Beard*, played the Opera House.

Though John Ellsler helped jump-start many prosperous theatrical careers, the Opera House seemed to cast its morose curse on his personal livelihood even before it opened on September 6, 1875. Cleveland had its share of skeptical citizens in the 1870s, many believing the city's size could not support a grand new theater, others predicting the needed money would never be obtained. As the date of the groundbreaking neared, the *Cleveland Leader* sought to silence cynics and disbelievers with this cheerful prediction: "Men may die, or an earthquake shake Cleveland into ruins, but the Opera House is as certain as anything which is yet undone."

Groundbreaking commenced about five weeks after the *Leader's* prognostication. With a construction budget of $100,000, Ellsler anticipated an 1874 opening. By February 1874, even though $70,000 had been spent, completion still required another $45,000; Ellsler suspended work until he raised the additional funds, much of it from his own savings. Five months later, the estimated completion cost had risen to $150,000, stopping construction a second time.

A concerned public offered supposedly constructive suggestions for saving the project, such as selling advance season tickets to defray the additional construction costs. Not surprisingly, the purchase of tickets for a season in jeopardy of ever existing did not capture the imagination of many Cleveland theatergoers. A new stock subscription, geared to the middle class rather than the wealthy, offered stock for $25 per share with payments in eight monthly installments of $3.12. Unfortunately, the middle class demonstrated little interest in investing each month in a new cultural center.

The theater's construction cost soared to $200,000, double the original budget. Part of the unexpected outlay included creating a 100-foot long by 20-foot wide entrance from Euclid Avenue, a magnificent passageway that included 4,000 pieces of marble and colored tile laid in cement. The costly entrance became necessary when the city failed to honor its promise to widen Fourth Street. Remaining in its narrow state, the street could not accommodate Opera House patrons arriving by carriage. In hindsight, the posh 101.5-foot Fourth Street frontage proved to be an unnecessary expense since theatergoers entering from Euclid Avenue never viewed the theater's exquisite blue sandstone front.

The additional expense, consuming Ellsler's entire life savings, still left the Opera House $12,000 in debt on its opening night. Despite the monetary disarray, the magnificence of the theater could not be disputed. Audiences marveled at intricate moldings and plasterwork situated throughout the theater, along with stairways finished with carved oak and walnut rails. Two thousand yards of carpet covered the floor, while overhead a superb 29-foot tall chandelier, spreading 14 feet in width, captivated theatergoers as they entered the lobby. Promoted as the largest prismatic fixture in the U.S., the chandelier weighted two tons and contained 325 gas jets.

The Euclid Avenue Opera House contained 634 seats downstairs, each upholstered in scarlet plush. The balcony seated 567 with an upstairs family circle providing another 437 seats. In total, the 1,638-seat capacity nearly doubled the size of the Academy of Music. *(Cleveland Public Library, Photographic Collection)*

Prior to the commercialization of the incandescent light bulb, theaters used gas jets as a source of lighting. At the Opera House, more than one thousand gas jets lighted the auditorium and stage. Electrical wiring preceded the invention of the light bulb, so the Opera House used 16 miles of intertwined electrical wire to connect the gas jets, thus permitting the use of electricity to simultaneously dim or brighten the integrated lights. Ten years later, the Opera House reengineered the lighting from gas to electricity.

The center of the expertly painted ceiling dome contained four figures representing tragedy, music, comedy, and poetry. The flat surface around the dome featured representations of playwright William Shakespeare, poet Lord Byron, and composers Gioachino Rossini and Wolfgang Amadeus Mozart. Cameos along the ceiling honored writer Johann Wolfgang von Goethe; poet and playwright Friedrich Schiller; poets William Cullen Bryant,

Dante Alighieri, and John Milton; Ludwig van Beethoven; and opera composers Giacomo Meyerbeer, Vincenzo Bellini, and Richard Wagner.

The stage dimensions, 78 feet wide and 55 feet deep, compared favorably to the finest theaters in the country; 21 traps distributed across the large stage helped create a variety of special effects. The impressive stage curtain contained 200 yards of red satin, 56 yards of heavy fringe, 300 yards of drapery cord, and 100 yards of velvet ribbon. A 33-foot high and 38-foot wide scenery curtain exhibited a painted scene of the old city of Damascus. A basement beneath the stage, measuring 18 feet high, 55 feet deep and 72 feet wide, housed stage machinery to permit the lowering of scenery. Twenty-one musicians could be seated in the orchestra pit.

Management boasted that each of the theater's 17 dressing rooms offered modern conveniences such as water, gas, and furniture. Male audience members enjoyed a distinctive amenity. During intermissions, gentlemen frequented the Opera House Bar, located in the theater's lobby; ladies characteristically remained in their seats to consume chocolates.

Unfortunately, the opening of the stunning new theater suffered from ill-fated timing that would typify Ellsler's future business decisions, as if an abysmal dark cloud settled overhead to adversely manipulate his once successful career. The Financial Panic of 1873, creating dire economic conditions for several years, negatively impacted the Opera House box office from the very first week. *The Plain Dealer* reported the initial week resulted in "audiences not as large as expected." Even though the quality of the productions remained excellent, attendance never grew to the level Ellsler required to reduce his debt.

The feeble economy eventually improved; nevertheless, Ellsler's misguided response to a growing business trend further strained his rapidly declining financial resources. Railroads revolutionized the business model for theater success, fostering tours with larger casts, vastly more intricate scenery and elaborate costumes literally tailor-made for each specific production. Theatergoers couldn't resist the promise of entertainment "presented here by the famous, faultless New York Company cast with four carloads of scenery." Producers enhanced their control over touring show standards and the public responded appreciatively to enticing claims such as "exactly as seen in New York."

Box office receipts soared when the Opera House presented exotic sounding out-of-state ensembles including the London Princess' Theater Company and Abbey's New York Park Theater Company. Clevelanders flocked to Amberg's New York Thalia Opera, Rudolph Aronson's New York Casino Opera, the Baggetto Grand Italian Opera Company, and numerous other

seemingly glamorous companies. Trains transported patrons from Ashtabula and Canton. Ships brought theatergoers from Sandusky and Norwalk. Everyone benefited except the time-honored stock companies now rapidly becoming outmoded relics.

The growing popularity of touring shows severely damaged Ellsler's financial position by radically reducing his portion of the theater's increased revenue. Owning both the playhouse and stock company, Ellsler previously retained most of the revenue from ticket sales. His share dwindled precariously

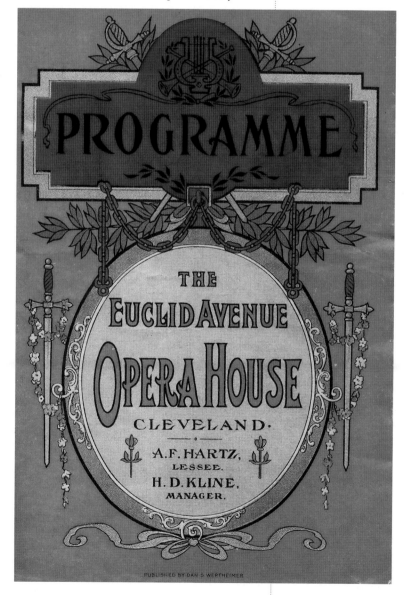

Euclid Avenue Opera House playbills in 1908 described bookings including George M. Cohan, the Ziegfeld Follies, Shakespearean actors Robert Mantell and Julia Marlow, and talking motion pictures.
(Alan Dutka collection)

as touring companies demanded the bulk of the theater's income. In 1878, Ellsler combined exceptional loyalty with catastrophic business judgment by leasing the old Academy of Music to provide his stock company additional employment as touring shows now dominated the Opera House. The ill-fated decision, requiring paychecks for 30 actors and 20 additional staff employees, drained what little remained of Ellsler's meager monetary resources. Sadly, Cleveland's pioneering theater manager gave up the Opera House at a sheriff's sale in 1879.

Mark Hanna, the powerful Cleveland industrialist and budding political star maker, purchased the Opera House under circumstances that created a captivating legend, most likely factual. Walking up Euclid Avenue, Hanna joined an unusually large crowd congregating at Fourth Street where the fate of the theater rested on the stroke on an auctioneer's gavel. The drama captured Hanna's curiosity; apparently on a whim, he raised the current $40,000 bid. A few seconds later, the surprised and proud Hanna owned the Opera House.

The exquisite playhouse, however, stagnated under the new ownership. Hanna, a wealthy capitalist, newspaper publisher, and bank executive, did not possess the time or expertise to manage a theater, and so he assigned the day-to-day operational tasks to Louis G. Hanna, his first cousin.

The dubious business relationship between the Hanna cousins shattered beyond repair when, on the evening of March 24, 1884, Louis creatively filled the Opera House with an event other than a theater production. By chance, Mark noticed a tough-looking crowd – not at all characteristic of the customary theatergoing audience – gathered at the Opera House door. Enterprising Louis had booked a professional wrestling match. Even though this match constituted an extraordinary wrestling competition, Louis badly misjudged Cousin Mark's lack of tolerance for grappling contests gracing the Opera House's hallowed stage. During the evening's match, challenger Duncan C. Ross defeated James H. McLaughlin, winning the prestigious American Collar-and-Elbow wrestling championship. Despite Louis promising the crowd a rematch, Mark's dislike for wrestling proved to be Detroit's gain. Mark Hanna refused another wrestling match in his theater, so McLaughlin regained his title from Ross the following month at the Detroit Opera House.

Cleveland industrialist Mark Hanna is pictured at the age of 43 in 1880, the year after he purchased the Euclid Avenue Opera House. *(Cleveland Press Collection, Cleveland State University)*

Following four years of mediocre results, Mark fired his relative, prompting the *New York Times* to report that Louis's demise resulted from "neglecting the business interests of the house."

Apparently still in awe of the magic created by a superb theatrical performance, Hanna hired a magician to replace his ineffective cousin. After a grueling 17-year touring career as a magician, Augustus Hartz selected Cleveland to establish a permanent home for his wife and two daughters. Hartz had never received a true opportunity to demonstrate his theater management skills. His lone previous attempt as a playhouse executive occurred at the newly constructed but ill-fated Park Theater on Public Square. The owners had advertised the Park as the country's only completely fireproof theater, but had evidently missed a few finer points about fire prevention. The showplace burned to the ground less than three months after its debut, and the spreading flames destroyed much of the neighboring Old Stone Church. Hanna, wasting no time in turning the unfortunate conflagration to his advantage, agreed to terms and hired Hartz after a 15-minute conversation.

Hartz began his management duties as the official 1883-1884 theatrical season ended. Lacking the funds to obtain a major attraction, Hartz displayed extraordinary creativity in keeping the theater operating and generating a reasonable profit. He combined a performance of the British import *H.M.S. Pinafore* (a less expensive booking because the U.S. ignored European copyrights at the time) with a special added attraction – his own act of captivating illusions.

Hanna had acquired an unanticipated competitive advantage by hiring a magician to manage his theater. When a void occurred in the bookings, or a show

The Opera House prospered for more than three decades under the astute management of Augustus Hartz.
(Cleveland Public Library, Photographic Collection)

required an added attendance boost, Hartz stepped in to exhibit his stage magic. To conclude the late-spring schedule, Hartz developed a version of *Uncle Tom's Cabin*, a production made financially possible when the head waiter at the Weddell House, a prominent downtown Cleveland Hotel, agreed to play Uncle Tom. At the closing of the Opera House in 1922, Hartz recalled in an interview that his 1884 *Uncle Tom* production cleared $3,000 in profit. "That propelled the theater and we didn't touch bottom again," he said.

Hartz continued to devise innovative bookings throughout his long Opera House career. In the 1890s, he created "Automatic Baseball," a niche summer attraction promising the use of electricity to develop "an actual and exact reproduction of Cleveland's games." He also displayed noted artwork in the lobby with viewing fees ranging from 15 to 25 cents. Hartz remained manager of the Opera House for 36 productive years.

Meanwhile, after his departure from the Opera House, John Ellsler concentrated on presenting stock company performances at the Academy of Music. As railroads threatened the stock company's existence, Abe Erlanger delivered another devastating blow. Klaw and Erlanger limited bookings of the latest popular plays to theaters controlled by their syndicate, a decision creating a Cleveland monopoly for the Opera House. Academy of Music actors and staff members had no opportunity to work with touring productions, and the theater could not create its own versions of newer shows. Ellsler continued to produce competent versions of classics, but many no longer in vogue with mainstream audiences. In effect, Erlanger helped destroy local stock companies across the country, including the very one for which he had hawked merchandise a decade earlier. Plummeting attendance forced the discouraged Ellsler to close the Academy of Music. Five months later, he failed for virtually the same reasons as manager of the rebuilt Park Theater on Public Square. Modern business methods in theatrical presentation relegated Ellsler, once a giant in Cleveland theater production, to nothing more than a faded relic of a bygone era.

The three consecutive setbacks crushed Ellsler's theatrical management aspirations. At the end of the Park Theater's 1887-1888 season, Ellsler joined Effie in New York. At an advanced age, Ellsler still needed a steady income

Left: The playbill design of 1916 helped welcome the Ziegfeld Follies, Irene Castle, John Barrymore, and 17 weeks of movies during the summer months. (Alan Dutka collection)

Right: Popular 1920 acts at the Opera House featured Eddie Cantor, Fannie Brice, and W. C. Fields in the Ziegfeld Follies and Ann Pennington in George White's Scandals. (Alan Dutka collection)

because of his financial misfortunes with the Opera House. Effie supplied her father with as much work as she could. In 1896, John Ellsler, along with Effie and her husband Frank Weston, returned to the Opera House with a repertoire including *Camille, As You Like It,* and *Romeo and Juliet.* John Ellsler also turned to Joe Haworth, his stock company's leading man in a previous generation, who provided roles for his former mentor in many successful productions.

John Ellsler and Joe Haworth both died in 1903, bringing painful closure to a chapter in Effie's life. The love scenes between Joe and Effie during their Opera House performances did not require acting, although their real-life relationship failed to progress since the couple did not receive family permission for marriage. Decades later, the two met again, rediscovering their youthful passions. The romantic attraction, however, remained doomed, this time because Effie had married a Broadway actor, and their union continued for 41 years until his death.

Although Haworth never entered into an official marriage, he had a daughter who, after a career as a Ziegfeld Follies showgirl, married dancer Eduardo Cansino. The husband-and-wife team formed a dance act playing the country's top vaudeville houses, including the Hippodrome and Palace theaters in Cleveland. Their marriage produced a daughter, Margarita Carmen Cansino, later known as Hollywood actress Rita Hayworth. Joe Haworth died before the birth of his famous granddaughter.

The Opera House prospered for eight years under the adept management of Gus Hartz, but the theater's triumphs came to a sudden end on October 29, 1892 when 11 different fires rocked downtown Cleveland in less than four hours, including an 8:39

a.m. alarm from inside the Opera House. Firefighters, tired and spread thin from their earlier morning battles, confronted the Opera House blaze with a damaged hose and equipment in need of repair. The theater faced almost certain destruction.

The Opera House roof collapsed only 21 minutes after the fire alarm's initial warning. A thundering crash of glass heralded the demise of the immense lobby chandelier. Cushioned seats, igniting a spectacular inferno, sealed the theater's frightful fate. Flames transformed the stage, once described by Edwin Booth as the finest ever constructed, into an unruly heap of twisted pipes, charred beams, and smoldering ashes. The blaze destroyed eight rooms of scenery and props, consuming the throne of Julius Caesar and the tomb of Juliet. The relentless inferno, while completely ruining the theater's interior, inflicted only slight damage to the exterior. The elegant Fourth Street entrance revealed no trace of the devastation inside. A city electrician speculated that faulty wiring ignited the blaze because an earlier examination revealed defective wire insulation. The city had actually condemned the entire system prior to the fire.

At the time of the fire, the Hanlon Brothers, a foremost international attraction in the second-half of the 19th Century, suffered the misfortune of being the Opera House attraction. Their spectacular presentations incorporated extensive use of special effects, illusions, scenery, and costumes. Audiences thrilled to viewing the beheading of knights, demons dropping from the clouds, locomotives speeding off the stage into the audience, balloon ascents, devastating cyclones, and a giant octopus devouring cast members. Hanlon's current extravaganza, on tour for only four weeks, had not yet been insured against fire.

Only 12 hours prior to the fateful blaze, insurance estimators had examined the Hanlon production in Cleveland to establish its value for fire protection. Adding to the misery, a previous series of fires inundating the downtown area just hours earlier had prompted performers and support teams to move their personal belongings from hotels into the illusionary safety of the Opera House. The fire consumed everything of value the company, its performers, and crews had transported to Cleveland.

Mark Hanna's initial reaction to the Opera House disaster exemplified his level-headed corporate judgment: "I am through with the theater business. I shall not rebuild." Realistically, Hanna never expected the Opera House to deliver financial returns comparable to his other business undertakings. With the exterior still intact, he relented and rebuilt the interior in a manner even more opulent than the original showplace. The playhouse's reopening on September 11, 1893, escalated into a major society event. No audience had ever paid as much to see a theatrical performance in Cleveland. Seats on the main floor, geared to the budgets of the moderate upper class, sold for $5; side boxes, filled with the city's snobbish society members, commanded between $50 and $250 per seat. Ladies dressed in lavish gowns and men wore tuxedos or their finest Sunday suits. Gus Hartz, ever mindful of who paid the theater's bills, designed an elaborate opening-night souvenir program with a faithful likeness of Mark Hanna prominently featured on the cover.

Following Cleveland society's pre-performance pageant, the headline theatrical presentation featured legendary actor Richard Mansfield in *Beau Brummell*. A mechanical problem prevented the curtain from descending at the first act's conclusion, depriving Mansfield of a customary curtain call. The infuriated actor stormed out of the theater, necessitating an understudy to assume his part in the second act.

Through the years, Opera House patrons enjoyed Shakespeare, grand opera, and the era's most successful plays and greatest actors. Lacking film or recording technologies, performances of 19th Century thespians are mostly relegated to the imaginations of theater historians. A few legendary Opera House entertainers are still recognizable even after the passing of a century: Sarah Bernhardt, George M. Cohan, Irving Berlin, Fred Astaire, Anna Held, Billie Burke, Marie Dressler, Lillian Russell, and Tyrone Power, Sr., are a few examples. Ironically, Effie Ellsler made several appearances as her father struggled in vain at the Academy of Music and Park Theater.

J. H. Haverly, the most influential producer of minstrel shows in the final quarter of the 19th Century, presented large troupes (often exceeding 100 members), accompanied by lavish scenery. In total, of the 26 minstrel companies that performed 76 separate engagements at the Opera House, Haverly presented 16. The inaccurate portrayal of black stereotypes is now fittingly considered highly offensive and demeaning. Yet many minstrel shows might be viewed as conservative compared with May Irwin's brand of entertainment. Capitalizing on a national trend in the 1890s, Irwin surfaced as one of America's leading "coon shouters." These white, female singers performed "coon songs" written to depict blacks as buffoons. During an 1899 Opera House appearance, Irwin's anthology of coon songs included "When Yo 'Ain't Got No Money Yo Needn't Come 'Round," "Dare's Sumpin' Bout Him Dat I Like," and "If I Only Had a Job."

In 1886, the New York Metropolitan Opera Company, just three years after its inaugural season, performed *Rienzi, Queen of Sheba, Lohengrin*, and *Tannhauser* at the Opera House. In 1899, the Met returned with performances of *the Barber of Seville, Carmen, La Traviata*, and *Faust*.

The colossal stage spectacle *Ben-Hur* made seven appearances at the Opera House between 1902 and 1920. Klaw and Erlanger conquered several formidable obstacles in transforming Lew Wallace's highly successful novel into a theatrical sensation. To simulate the crucial chariot race, two teams of four horses galloped on a pair of treadmills as background scenery moved to create the illusion of actual motion. The appearance of Jesus Christ, a sensitive issue in the first decade of the 20th Century, took the form of a beam of white light. William Young, once an aspiring actor in John Ellsler's stock company, rose to prominence for transforming novels into

stage plays. His creativity helped transfer the *Ben-Hur* novel into an enormous stage success.

With a mammoth cast of 300 people, *Ben-Hur* offered local residents an opportunity to achieve five minutes of stage fame by acting as extras in the immense production. One Clevelander took full advantage of the opportunity. An East High School student conditionally landed a part in the *Ben-Hur* cast provided his mother would allow him to miss classes during a Wednesday matinee performance. Realizing the impossibility of this task, he coaxed his grandmother into writing the crucial letter of permission. Somehow, grandma misinterpreted her grandson's request as permission to remain after school to participate in a student recital, and she proudly cooperated in authoring the essential letter. Since she could

The stage production of *Ben-Hur*, supporting a cast of 300 individuals, relied on a pool of local extras. At the Opera House, Adolphe Menjou launched a distinguished 47-year acting career as an extra in this blockbuster stage epic. *(Alan Dutka collection)*

only speak and write in French, the budding thespian translated the letter into permission to take part in the theater production. His triumphant performance led to additional Opera House roles as an extra in *The Pit* and *Romeo and Juliet*, the latter featuring the early-20th-Century dream team of E. H. Sothern and Julia Marlowe. These performances launched the career of debonair, man-about-town film actor Adolphe Menjou. His 47 years in motion pictures included an Academy Award nomination for *The Front Page* in 1931. Menjou also hosted two television programs in the 1950s.

Beginning in 1908, the Opera House presented 13 of the first 14 editions of Ziegfeld's Follies. Clevelanders witnessed the grooming of future stars W. C. Fields, Fanny Brice, Will Rogers, Eddie Cantor, Sophie Tucker, Ed Wynn, the Dolly Sisters, Bert Williams, Leon Errol, Ina Claire, Marilyn Miller, Gus Van and Joe Schenck, Ann Pennington, Marion Davies, and Mae Murray. Irving Berlin and Victor Herbert contributed lyrics and music. Among the songs introduced in these editions are the standards: "Shine on Harvest Moon"; "By the Light of the Silvery Moon"; "You'd be Surprised"; "Row, Row, Row"; "How 'Ya Gonna Keep 'Em Down on The Farm"; and Ziegfeld's anthem, "A Pretty Girl is Like a Melody."

The Opera House also played a prominent local role in three ill-fated attempts to depose the powerful B. F. Keith vaudeville empire. In 1906, Klaw & Englander tested Keith's resolve by presenting a four-week summer vaudeville program. Keith reacted immediately with newspaper advertisements claiming the new Opera House competition charged higher prices for old and tired former Keith acts. Keith correctly predicted, "It's going to be mighty hard work to

fool Cleveland theatergoers for even four weeks." In 1912, the Shubert brothers launched the first of their two attacks on the rival Keith organization with a summer vaudeville season at the Opera House. After announcing the Keith Hippodrome would close for a 14-week summer break, management immediately reopened the theater with a full summer of vaudeville.

In addition to taking aim at the Opera House, Keith also lambasted the new store-front motion picture theaters: "Don't ruin your health in stuffy, store picture shows when, for the same price, you can enjoy much better entertainment in a well ventilated, cool, clean, safe theater." The Keith organization proudly announced that 30,246 Clevelanders paid to see Hippodrome vaudeville during the first five days of the competition. Once again, Keith dominated summer vaudeville in Cleveland.

In 1921, the Shuberts returned with a more aggressive assault on Keith's vaudeville realm. The Opera House benefited from a substantial remodeling and redecorating effort as it launched Cleveland's venue for the new Shubert vaudeville circuit. Improvements included exterior renovations, new box offices, beautifully recovered seats, and new carpeting and painting. The Opera House played 12 weeks of Shubert Vaudeville before the productions moved to the newly opened Ohio Theater for 16 additional weeks. After a summer break, the State Theater housed Shubert Vaudeville for 23 weeks. The Shuberts signed rising star Fred Allen along with established performers Nora Bayes, Marie Dressler, and Lew Fields, although most shows highlighted unknown performers who remained unknown, causing the Shuberts' effort to fail within two years. Before the decade ended, the growing popularity of movies accomplished what neither Klaw and Englander nor the Shubert brothers could achieve. The Keith vaudeville organization died in 1929.

In 1919, the comedy *Daddies* featured a supporting role for a 32-year-old actor in one of his first stage performances. Sixty-eight years later, George Abbot celebrated his 100th birthday in Cleveland by directing a revival of his 1926 hit *Broadway*. Abbot's prolific career included writing, directing, and producing numerous Broadway shows and motion pictures. Among his many successes, Abbott wrote and directed the Broadway versions of *The Pajama Game* and *Damn Yankees*, and then produced, directed, and authored the screenplays for the film versions of both shows. Abbot lived past his 107th birthday, remaining active his entire life.

Similar to most vaudeville and legitimate theaters, the Opera House initially treated movies as a peculiar curiosity. Motion pictures, introduced as a minor part of the 1909 summer vaudeville season, consisted of one-reel novelties without plots or characters. By 1913, these hot-weather attractions had matured to include recognizable narratives such as *The Scarlet Letter, David Copperfield,* and *The Last Days of Pompeii.* As motion pictures increased in stature, prestigious films commanding higher prices and reserved-seats migrated from motion picture playhouses to legitimate theaters. In 1917, the Opera House presented D. W. Griffith's pioneering *The Birth of a Nation* for eight weeks. The popular stage play *Way Down East* delighted Opera House audiences during eight engagements between 1898 and 1908. The 1921 motion picture version enjoyed a record-breaking ten-week run at the Opera House. D. W. Griffith, the legendary director, and Lillian Gish, his leading lady, appeared in person to commemorate the 100th showing of the film at the Opera House.

In the first three months of 1922, the Opera House remained in operation every week, still attracting large audiences for performances by Ethel Barrymore, Will Rogers, Otis Skinner, Elsie Janis, William Gillette, Elsie Ferguson, and other first-rate entertainers. Even so, Playhouse Square's new Hanna and Ohio theaters doomed the Opera House's existence by successfully securing the vast majority of prestigious new shows. On April 2, 1922, the Opera House presented a closing tribute to Gus Hartz. The following morning wrecking balls began demolishing the historic theater, paving the way for a Kresge store on the site currently occupied by the Pickwick and Frolic entertainment complex.

THE DREW-BARRYMORE LEGACY

London-born Louise Lane, whose father and mother both acted on the stage, made her professional debut at the age of 12 months playing a crying baby, not always responding to the proper cues. In America, she matured into a distinguished actress and theater manager. Irish-born actor John Drew, Lane's third husband, immigrated to Boston at a young age. Through marriage with the Barrymore family, John and Louise's offspring produced four additional generations of stage and screen celebrities, including Drew Barrymore, their great-great granddaughter.

John Drew died before the Opera House opened; Louise Lane Drew appeared four times between 1881 and 1896. The offspring of John and Louise included Louisa Drew, John Drew, Jr., and Georgina Drew.

Louise also adopted Sidney Drew after her husband's death. The four children each contributed to the family's acting heritage:

Although not an actress, Louisa Drew gave birth to actress Georgie Drew Mendum who graced the Broadway stage 12 times.

John Drew, Jr., a renowned stage and screen actor, performed in ten productions at the Opera House. Louise Drew, his daughter, developed into an accomplished actress whose career included 13 Broadway appearances.

Georgina Drew made two Opera House appearances. Her marriage to stage actor Maurice Barrymore united the Drew and Barrymore families.

Sidney Drew acted in an Opera House drama in 1889.

Maurice Barrymore performed at the Opera House three times. The union of Georgina and Maurice produced two sons, Lionel and John Barrymore, and a daughter, Ethel Barrymore. Grandmother Louise Lane Drew emerged as the driving force behind the acting careers of Lionel, John, and Ethel, all of whom expressed interests in livelihoods other than acting.

Lionel Barrymore, a character actor in movies for 40 years, never appeared at the Opera House.

John Barrymore, a star of stage, as well as silent and sound motion pictures, performed twice at the Opera House. His second wife, poet Blanche Oelrichs, gave birth to actress Diana Barrymore. John Drew Barrymore, Jr., the son of John Barrymore and his third wife, Dolores Costello, performed in films and on television.

Ethel Barrymore's distinguished stage career, including seven engagements at the Opera House, enhanced as well as perpetuated the family's acting tradition. Ethel Barrymore Colt, her daughter, enjoyed an acting and singing career.

Members of the two eminent families acted together twice at the Opera House. In 1881, the mother and son-in-law combination of Mrs. John Drew and Maurice Barrymore appeared in

Top: John Drew established one branch of the most famous acting family in American stage history.

Bottom: Ethel Barrymore, the granddaughter of John Drew, enhanced the family's reputation on both the stage and screen. *(Cleveland Public Library, Photographic Collection)*

Left: John Barrymore and Dolores Costello pose for a picture on their wedding day, November 24, 1928. *(Cleveland Public Library, Photographic Collection)*

Right: John Barrymore and Dolores Costello admire John Drew Barrymore, Jr. The infant, born June 4, 1932, became the father of screen actress Drew Barrymore. *(Cleveland Public Library, Photographic Collection)*

The Rivals. In 1897, uncle John Drew and niece Ethel Barrymore performed in *Rosemary.*

Drew Barrymore is the daughter of John Drew Barrymore, Jr. and Ildiko Jaid Mako, his fourth wife. John Barrymore III,

Drew Barrymore's half-brother, is a former actor now embarked in a second career as a software developer. His birth resulted from the marriage of John Drew Barrymore, Jr. and Cara Williams, an actress whose skills warranted both Academy and Emmy award nominations.

A TROMBONIST HARBORING MILLION-DOLLAR IDEAS

The smooth ride in today's automobiles is the direct result of the inventive spirit of a former Opera House trombonist. Many aspiring performers supplement their meager artistic incomes by waiting on tables or toiling at similar tasks. Cleveland inventor Claud Foster reversed the long-established process. His 11-year stint playing trombone in the Opera House orchestra subsidized research leading to various contraptions, including the shock absorber, designed for the burgeoning automobile market.

Foster, born in 1872, quit school at the age of 11 to work on his father's Brooklyn, Ohio, farm. Before his 15th birthday, he demonstrated an uncanny ability to make excellent business decisions. Foster

convinced his father to plant a very early crop of potatoes, and, for the first time in years, no killing frost hindered early planted vegetables. The initial harvest, commanding a premium price, allowed his father to pay longstanding bills.

Five years later, Foster opened a small machine shop on East Ninth Street. When the Opera House reopened in 1893 after the devastating fire, Foster obtained a position as a trombonist, earning $14 per week playing at two matinees and six evening performances. Still interested in mechanical tinkering, a friend offered Foster space in his grinding shop on Fourth Street so Foster could quickly alternate between his trombone playing and research activities.

Fourteen years later, Foster introduced a musical automobile horn powered by exhaust gasses. He offered the creatively named Gabriel's Horn in four varieties, geared to customers' differing monetary budgets and musical tastes. A two-tone horn sold for $18, with three tones for $25, four tones for $35, and a magnificent 10-tone horn priced at $200. His innovative novelty created a worldwide sensation resulting in purchases by King Edward VII of England, Emperor Nicholas II of Russia, and King Alfonso XIII of Spain. Foster's invention yielded solid sales in most European countries with the notable exception of Germany. Kaiser Wilhelm II, so enamored by the clever gadget, issued an edict forbidding anyone in Germany, except himself, from owning a Gabriel Horn.

The invention of the snubber, the first commercial automobile shock absorber, boosted Foster into the circle of millionaire industrialists. Between 1920 and 1925, his company manufactured 75 percent of the world's shock absorbers. In 1924, Foster paid $821,313 in income taxes, the largest amount of any Ohio taxpayer. Foster refused an offer of $10 million for his business, claiming expiring patents substantially reduced the value of the corporation. He rejected attempts to negotiate a lower asking price because, in his opinion, the suitor had already demonstrated too much incompetence. Foster later sold his company for what he considered the more realistic price of $4 million. He remained chairman of the business until his retirement in 1928 at the age of 55.

Foster distributed most of his fortune to educational institutions, hospitals, churches, and charities. He contributed the funds to build Fenn College's Mechanical Engineering Building, noting that he personally related to the school's mandatory work-study program where students "work hard and earn their

Left: At the age of 56, former Opera House trombonist Claud Foster still enjoyed participating in musical gigs. His 1929 performance at a fancy dinner-dance costume party in Pasadena captured a first place award for most original costume.

Right: Twenty years later, in a more dignified setting, Foster inspects equipment in Fenn College's new Foster Mechanical Engineering Building named in his honor. *(Cleveland State University, Cleveland Press Collection)*

own way." Seven hundred small churches, unable to pay for organs, received them as gifts from Foster. In 1952, he invited guests to a Hotel Statler dinner, promising each "the surprise of their lives." After dinner, he distributed $4 million to 16 nonprofit organizations. Foster told the group, "I have no more use for the money. You can take it all, but leave me my friends." After retirement, Foster occupied his remaining 37 years tinkering with new inventions, playing golf, and hunting. Foster's $3,500 home in Willowick, located at 30333 Lakeshore Boulevard, still exists and is on the National Register of Historic Places.

Many of the buildings constructed because of Foster's generosity are no longer in existence. Cleveland State University demolished the mechanical engineering building and Case Western University razed a Foster dormitory. The life of the Claud Foster Surgical Research Laboratory at Saint Luke's Medical Center ended with the closing of the hospital. Seeking little publicity or recognition during his life, Foster's legacy as one of Cleveland's most unusual and benevolent industrialists is not widely known or appreciated today.

A VIOLIN PLAYER'S CENTURY-OLD BUSINESS

Asher D. Bonfoey, a violinist in the Opera House orchestra, transformed a hobby into a business still prospering more than a century later. Bonfoey planted the seed for his new endeavor by designing a frame to display a silhouette valentine he had given his wife. Admiring friends desired similar work, and an escalating demand inspired the founding of a husband-and-wife custom framing company. Asher designed frames, and his spouse Della created fabric mats. Weary of listening to Asher's violin practice, Della moved her creative efforts to the basement of their home located on Woodland Avenue near East 55th Street.

In 1893, the couple relocated their business to a building on the west side of East Ninth Street, about one block north of Euclid Avenue. Asher's insistence on excellence attracted and retained a prestigious client list, and his membership in a bridge group with John D. Rockefeller generated even more business contacts. Through John D.'s efforts, Asher added Henry Ford to the company's registry of satisfied customers. Bonfoey moved to the fifth floor of Fourth Street's Buckeye Building

after a 1903 fire destroyed the East Ninth Street site. In the first third of the 20th Century, demonstrating expertise in framing beyond pictures, the company emerged as the largest provider of silk and velvet coffin liners between New York and Chicago.

Asher, searching for an eventual successor, hired George Moore in 1928. The 21-year-old aspiring Ohio Bell revenue accountant redirected his career from accounting to picture framing because, in the words of his son, he grew tired of sitting around moving numbers. The 11-year management transition culminated with George purchasing the company upon Asher and Della's retirement in 1939.

Bonfoey's client list expanded with the addition of industrialist John L. Severance, politician Frances P. Bolton, publisher Thomas Vail, the wife of industrialist Francis F. Prentiss, and William M. Milliken, the director of the Cleveland Museum of Art. The Bonfoey Company reached its peak employment of 32 full-time craftsmen just prior to the Great Depression. While sales expanded after World War II, employment did not keep pace since automation reduced time-consuming labor. During the 1930s, the core clientele changed from wealthy private citizens to many of Northeast Ohio's premier corporations, including Warner & Swasey, TRW, Hanna Mining, Oglebay Norton, Firestone Tire & Rubber, Addressograph Multigraph, Webb C. Ball, and Sterling Lindner Davis.

George Moore's 16-year-old son Richard helped his father wrap merchandise and answer telephone calls during a busy Christmas season. Richard continued his assistance for five more years during his high school and college breaks. He entered Wittenberg University in Springfield, Ohio. After one year, Richard transferred to Hillsdale College in Michigan. Then, completing his college work at Abilene Christian College, he majored in business with minors in political science and art. Richard's proficiency as a college baseball pitcher resulted in a season with the St. Louis Cardinal's farm system. He briefly contemplated opening a men's cowboy clothing store in Texas after his college graduation, but somehow knew his future existed in his father's business. In 1955, Richard accepted a full-time position with Bonfoey. He studied law in the evenings for three years until he complained to a professor about an examination grade. His interest in law ended when the professor complimented him on his intelligence but told him he made a lousy law student.

George Gund personally brought his paintings to Bonfoey's workplace for framing. The influential banker impressed George and Richard by always remembering their first names. After one of Gund's visits, the Buckeye Building elevator operator mentioned to the Moores that Gund, before entering the Bonfoey Company, always asked the first names of the two gentlemen operating the framing company on the fifth floor.

Through the years, the company participated in framing projects involving an Eskimo totem pole, a wedding gown complete with veil, and a pair of pink bloomers. One client hired Bonfoey to frame a variety of Civil War memorabilia. The customer attempted to expand his collection to include the Civil War cannon residing on Public Square. Equipped with a truck, he and three helpers lifted the cannon into the vehicle during a busy lunch hour. Police recovered the cannon where it still rests on the square to this day. The Moores lost their client in the ordeal, since he never appeared again even though some of his framed treasures waited for his pickup. Another client arrived with his life's belongings including clothes, jewelry, and letters, along with a picture of a crypt. He commissioned the company to create a similar five-foot-long by three-foot-wide crypt capable of holding himself and all of his worldly possessions. The client loathed his family and had no intention of sharing any possessions after his death.

Quality work is critical in creating an excellent reputation, but logistics can also play an important role. Richard Moore once framed an extremely large Indian headdress, and found the nine-foot finished product did not fit in the Buckeye Building elevator. Moore lowered his work five stories from a window onto a waiting delivery truck. Another client, recovering from a heart attack in a local hospital, had Moore use a lift to hoist six or seven pictures three floors to the client's hospital room window so he could select his favorite pictures.

George and Richard attended a Cleveland Browns football game in the fall 1961. Walking up East Ninth Street after the contest, they noticed smoke and flames pouring from a building on Prospect Avenue. As they approached the fire, the two witnessed the destruction of their business. A jewelry shop owner on the same floor had neglected to turn off a motor when he left for the weekend, inadvertently causing the fire when the motor overheated. The blaze destroyed Bonfoey's entire company except for a safe, cash register, letter opener, corporate stamp, and a stool. Along with their extensive inventory of frames and matting, the fire consumed valuable artwork from current projects for Stouffer's and the Higbee and Halle department stores. The company temporarily moved three floors to the vacated Andres Cafeteria site for two years. After six decades on Fourth Street, Bonfoey then relocated to 1710 Euclid Avenue, where the company still resides today.

In addition to framing, the company expanded to offer restoration and repair services for paintings and textiles. In the mid-1980s, the city of Cleveland hired Bonfoey to clean and restore one of Archibald Willard's famous *Spirit of '76* paintings. Richard began displaying works of Cleveland artists, and the company gained a reputation as an excellent art gallery.

Richard became president in 1971 and still owns and manages the company today. George remained involved in the organization until his death in 1993. Asked about the resolution of business differences occurring between Richard as company president and his still-active father, Richard commented, "You never win battles against your father."

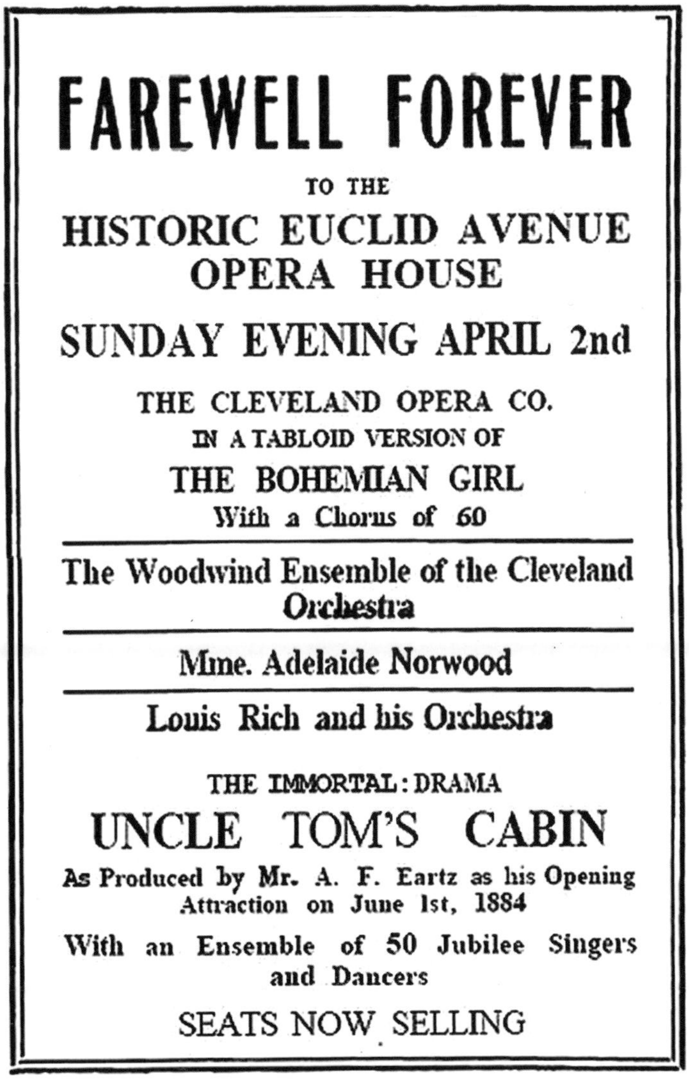

FAREWELL FOREVER

TO THE

HISTORIC EUCLID AVENUE OPERA HOUSE

SUNDAY EVENING APRIL 2nd

THE CLEVELAND OPERA CO.
IN A TABLOID VERSION OF
THE BOHEMIAN GIRL
With a Chorus of 60

The Woodwind Ensemble of the Cleveland Orchestra

Mme. Adelaide Norwood

Louis Rich and his Orchestra

THE IMMORTAL : DRAMA
UNCLE TOM'S CABIN
As Produced by Mr. A. F. Eartz as his Opening
Attraction on June 1st, 1884
With an Ensemble of 50 Jubilee Singers
and Dancers

SEATS NOW SELLING

Clevelanders flocked to the Opera House for 47 years until the final curtain came down on April 2, 1922. *(Alan Dutka collection)*

Chapter III
Market Memories

TIMELINE

1856   The newly constructed Central Market bordered Fourth Street.

1891   A private company launched the competing Sheriff Street Market.

1924   Cleveland leaders called for the replacement of the Central Market.

1930   Fire destroyed much of the Sheriff Street Market.

1949   Fire consumed the 93-year-old Central Market.

1950   Vendors from the ruined Central Market reopened the former
        Sheriff Street Market, naming the new facility the New Central Market.

1988   Construction of the Gateway sports complex forced razing
        the New Central Market.

Shoppers today cannot conceive of groceries forcefully escaping from their packaging. Yet before the era of cellophane, an errant duck or wayward chicken occasionally raced down a streetcar aisle with its owner in hot pursuit. Cleveland's two downtown markets offered a wide assortment of living poultry. After a customer chose a handsome bird, the vendor wrapped the selection in a piece of newspaper and tied its feet together. The fowl's fate became the purchaser's responsibility, sometimes to the chagrin of streetcar passengers dodging attempted chicken escapes or a mailman eluding harassment from a cantankerous goose. Fenced-in city yards imprisoned live geese prior to their becoming leading attractions at magnificent Christmas or Easter feasts. Ineffective city laws banned keeping living livestock in homes, and complaints about unsupervised fowl roaming through neighborhoods merely led to birds enjoying their final hours in attics or basements.

Downtown markets evolved soon after Cleveland's founding. Local politicians viewed constructing and regulating markets a civic responsibility akin to maintaining roads or building bridges. East Fourth Street bordered at least one major marketplace for 133 years. The city-owned Central Market and privately held Sheriff Street Market stood, almost side-by-side, in direct competition for more than two generations.

Five major streets terminating at the Central Market created daily traffic delays and backups. At the bottom of the photograph, East Fourth Street (left) and Ontario Street (center) converge on the market. Directly to the left of Fourth Street is the remaining piece of the Sheriff Street Market following a 1930 fire. Bolivar Road, mostly obscured by the Sheriff Street Market, runs west and dead ends into Fourth Street. At the top left, Woodland Avenue ends at the Central Market; Broadway Avenue terminates from the top center.
(Cleveland State University, Bruce Young collection)

In the 1920s, Central Market vendors, overflowing onto sidewalks and streets, created fire hazards and traffic congestion as automobile traffic increased.
(Alan Dutka collection)

The Central Market (1856 - 1949)

In 1839, Cleveland operated a downtown market on Michigan Street, a road later obliterated by the construction of the Terminal Tower. The city rapidly outgrew this meager facility, constructing the larger Central Market in 1856. The boundaries of the new market included East Fourth and Ontario streets, Bolivar Road and Broadway, Woodland and Eagle avenues. Cleveland paid $1,500 to obtain the land.

The Central Market experienced a sluggish beginning. For reasons obscured by time, vendors preferred the old Michigan Street location, refusing to relocate to the new facility. Even the hucksters favored the old site. These enterprising business people purchased produce at markets, reselling their stock from horse and wagons at greatly increased prices as they traveled through Cleveland's neighborhoods. Other hucksters, purchasing produce from nearby farmers, sold vegetables, fruits, eggs, and butter near the market at prices lower than those charged by the market vendors.

The City, failing in its mission to encourage use of the Central Market, offered a bargain rent of only 50 cents per week per stand. When this liberal fee did not lure dealers from Michigan Street, Cleveland passed an ordinance forbidding the use of any market except the new Central Market. Ingenious lawyers, discovering loopholes in the ordinance, inspired both merchants and hucksters to raise money in defense of their comrades arrested for using the old facility. Two years later, the Central Market finally attracted a reasonable number of tenants.

The Civil War interrupted mercantile trade when the Union converted the market into a temporary barracks. In 1867, as Cleveland's population continued its rapid acceleration, the city rebuilt and expanded the Central Market to accommodate 100 stands for fish, meat, and vegetables.

In its 1890s heyday, the Central Market's 300 retailers serviced 100,000 weekly customers. Horse radish grinders congregated near the Broadway Avenue area; the opposite end housed sellers of household notions, yard goods, tin ware, and crockery. In between, dealers peddled meats, fish, produce, butter, cheese, and flowers. As customers progressed down the market's aisles, feisty vendors attempted to outdo their competition with cries of "fresh apples," "fresher apples," "really fresh apples," and "cheap and fresh apples." Outside the market, farmers sold cabbages, onions, and potatoes from wagons backed to the Fourth Street curb. In the winter, these hardy merchants kept warm by using kerosene torches or setting fire to unwanted boxes. On Saturday night, the sidewalks overflowed with pitchmen hawking pain killers, nerve tonics, and magic rings,

Gobbling turkeys, quacking ducks, and squawking geese all performed their swan songs at the Central Market on November 25, 1931. The following day, Clevelanders devoured the birds during Thanksgiving dinners.
(Cleveland State University, Cleveland Press *Collection)*

as card sharks, shell game artists, and pickpockets perfected their trades.

Market sellers endured 18-hour days and grueling physical labor. Setup and preparation began long before customers arrived. After hauling heavy boxes and crates filled with food from basement coolers to ground-floor sales stands, retailers routinely stood for hours at a time selling their merchandise. The urge to operate a business often outweighed the profession's harsh disadvantages. First-generation immigrants sought a ground-floor opportunity to prosper; others began their careers at early ages, sometimes in the third or fourth grade, carrying on family traditions started by parents or grandparents.

A typical selling day began with grocery store owners, eager to stock their businesses, arriving as the market opened at 6:00 a.m., and household servants came early to procure food to satisfy their employer's daily household requirements. Market vendors devoted the remainder of the day catering to the general public. In the initial years, shoppers walked to the market, some enduring distances of 40 blocks. Others arrived in a horse and buggy. Parents and grandparents entertained their young offspring, pulling them in makeshift wagons used to transport groceries back to their homes. Streetcars eventually made the trip easier as various routes terminated at or near the market. In time, chauffeur-driven automobiles arrived with ladies adorned in mink coats.

The 20th Century witnessed a sharp rise in the wholesale market business. Farmers increasingly sold their food to commission merchants, located near the market, rather than directly to vendors. Entrepreneurs also operated imaginative wholesale meat businesses on street curbs. The resellers purchased sides of beef at neighborhood

slaughterhouses, hung the meat on racks near the street, and sold their goods to market butchers. Experienced wholesalers drove hard bargains, subsequently reducing the Central Market merchants' profit margins. The growth of neighborhood butcher shops and grocery stores created additional formidable competition. In 1850, only 50 grocery stores operated in the city of Cleveland; by 1917, the number had increased to 2,575. A new generation of shoppers demonstrated less loyalty to the downtown markets, no longer reigning as the primary source for the city's daily supply of fresh fruit, meat, and dairy products.

At the beginning of the 20th Century, nearly half of U.S. households used an icebox to keep food cold. Most of the

Market vendors used sidewalks and streets as extended workplaces, as illustrated in this 1940 photograph. *(Cleveland State University, Cleveland* Press *Collection)*

In 1940, traffic converged on the Central Market from every direction. During market hours, three police officers directed crisscrossing automobiles, streetcars, and trucks. East Fourth Street is to the left of the market building. *(Cleveland State University, Cleveland* Press *Collection)*

Merchants selling live poultry expanded from the Central Market building onto nearby streets. *(Cleveland Public Library, Photographic Collection)*

remaining families had no cold storage capability of any kind. In either case, housewives depended on downtown markets for their daily supply of perishable foods. As the century progressed, the growing popularity of home refrigerators further hampered market sales.

Home refrigerators actually existed before the turn of the century. In 1900, George Worthington's hardware store in the Warehouse District sold four burgeoning brands: Cold Storage, Glacier, Ice King, and Defender. The general public resisted using refrigerators because of their annoying habit of occasionally blinding, burning, or even killing their owners. Leaks in refrigerators, emitting toxic and flammable gas, created well-publicized fatal accidents, petrifying prospective purchasers. Some owners relegated their potentially lethal appliance from a place of prominence in the kitchen to a backyard hideaway. In

1929, safety concerns dissipated with the introduction of Freon, a colorless, odorless, nonflammable, and noncorrosive gas. By 1935, Americans had purchased eight million new Freon-equipped refrigerators, even in the depths of the Great Depression. Freon's endangerment to the Earth's ozone layer did not become an issue until a later generation.

The Central Market, endangered by these new competitive threats, declined in physical appearance and functionality. As far back as 1890, a few civic leaders initiated an earnest movement to upgrade or replace the building, largely because the structure lacked adequate sanitary facilities. Despite the Cleveland Board of Trade not viewing inadequate hygiene or cleanliness as serious problems, public complaints intensified the momentum to raze the old market house. Nevertheless, the resilient Central Market lived on even as three generations of politicians struggled

George B. Gehring's Central Market grocery store attracted its usual large crowd in 1946 *(Cleveland State University, Cleveland* Press *Collection)*

in vain to end its existence.

In 1924, Cleveland's leaders deemed the building "no longer adequate as a market structure" and declared it "must be abandoned in a few years." Sixteen years later, since the obsolete structure lacked running water and refrigeration, members of a special political committee concluded the antiquated building should be razed.

Originally, the market's location occupied a relatively out-of-the-way section of the city. Cleveland's growth and changing street usage patterns eventually placed the market literally in the middle of the intersection of Ontario Street and Broadway and Woodland avenues, one of the city's busiest traffic locations. Fire and traffic authorities warned of potential dangers created by the market's peculiar location. Cleveland's postmaster claimed traffic congestion, caused by the Central

Market, slowed or prevented 465 mail trips each day to the nearby main post office.

In 1940, Cleveland spruced up the market cosmetically by replacing the floor, rebuilding stands, repairing the roof, and painting the outside. Even so, the building's exterior still generated descriptions including "eyesore," "traffic bottleneck," and "health menace," and the interior invoked images of "dimly lit," "grimy walls," and "rickety floors."

The Health Department demanded meat products be kept under constant refrigeration, although not one refrigerated counter existed in the entire market. To circumvent the problem, merchants periodically replenished meats from cold storage facilities located at Fourth Street and Bolivar Road. Another health regulation required hot and cold water at every meat stand to clean counters, cutting instruments, and meat blocks. Since no such capability existed, vendors lugged water from the market's single water faucet. The market, had it been a private enterprise, would have surely been closed by the Health Department. But in 1939 the Central Market produced a profit of $41,208 for Cleveland, one of the few profitable city departments. Despite the obvious drawbacks, about 75,000 shoppers each week depended on the market for daily supplies of meat, fresh produce, and dairy products. Since closing the market would put more than 300 vendors out of business, logic dictated constructing a new market prior to closing the existing one.

Spirited discussions regarding the market's ultimate destiny continued. One suggestion, formulated in 1944, involved converting the unused lower level of the Lorain-Carnegie Bridge into a public market house. A strong selling point of this scheme revolved around a perceived reduction in the market's rat population. Proponents of the plan believed rodents would have more difficulty reaching market stands located in the lower portion of a bridge compared with stands situated on downtown streets. Central Market critics misplayed the rodent issue since market employees had been setting 185 rat traps each evening with a paltry average catch of only five per night.

In 1946, Clevelanders approved a bond issue for a new market, but three years later, this already authorized capital improvement did not even warrant inclusion in the city's five-year development plan. The Central Market appeared almost certain to enter the second half of the 20th Century without a verdict about its future.

Then, on December 17, 1949, flames consumed the entire 93-year-old structure, finally accomplishing in two hours what political bickering had failed to achieve in

The disastrous 1949 Central Market blaze destroyed this fire truck trapped on Fourth Street. *(Cleveland Public Library, Photographic Collection)*

60 years. The huge roof plunged with a thunderous crash into the blazing inferno below. Heat seared the faces of valiant firemen and inquisitive spectators. The walls, collapsing inward, fortunately minimized potentially immense traffic problems on Broadway Avenue and Ontario Street.

A westerly wind fanned leaping flames across Fourth Street, creating intense heat that caused electric power line insulation to burst into flames, plunging the area into darkness. Three firemen suffered burns as they connected hose lines to a Fourth Street hydrant. Flames from a falling trolley wire destroyed a fire truck parked

The Central Market lay in ruins after the catastrophic 1949 fire. Ontario Street is to the left, East Fourth Street to the right. *(Cleveland Public Library, Photographic Collection)*

on the street. Sixty-year-old Edward Pesek fractured his right ankle as he leaped from a second-story window of his Fourth Street apartment above Peppers Café, a popular hangout soon to be reduced to a parking lot. The fire completely destroyed the Glenville Paper Company, another occupant of Fourth Street.

The market inferno, providing a fleeting source of entertainment for thousands of gawkers and a sense of relief among politicians, also deprived merchants of lucrative holiday sales, creating severe financial burdens. Even worse, insurance companies, considering the building an indisputable fire trap, had established exorbitant premiums. Consequently, few merchants carried fire insurance on their property or merchandise.

The *Plain Dealer* prophesized, "Cleveland will be a better city because of the cleansing properties of fire." In contrast, the merchants, many of whom had toiled at the market nearly their entire lives, suffered heartbreaking feelings of grief and abandonment. Vera Weimer, the wife of a pork seller, poignantly described her reaction to the fire: "It was as though part of our own lives had been reduced to ashes."

Many other merchants joined in Vera's

feelings of despair. Seventy-four-year-old Charles Eisemann had devoted 52 years of his life to selling sausage at the market. He first opened his stand on February 6, 1897. His wife Lillie assisted him after their marriage in 1900, and their six children all pitched in to help as junior and senior high school students. Rudolph, one of Charles's sons, progressed to a business partner after working with his father for 28 years. In its last years, the stand generated monthly sales of between $2,500 and $3,000 while Eisemann paid only $55 in rent. After viewing the charred remains of a cash register, two scales, and a slicing machine, Charles compared his grief to losing an old friend.

An ambitious Johnny Koenigshoff started his Central Market career in 1897 at the age of 17, growing the business in part by purchasing drinks for patrons of nearby saloons. Gifts to employees of the Cleveland Provision Company wholesale house assured the finest cuts of meat in return. Hard work and astute public relations propelled Koenigshoff to his place as the largest operator in the market at the time of the fire.

The market had many other veteran dealers when the blaze occurred. Seventy-six-year-old Ben Whitmore, a pork seller, began his stint at age 20. C. W. McDonnell, age 70, sold butter and eggs for 50 years, his grandson later joining him in the business. Ed Hancy, at age 73, had accumulated 49 years dealing in pork. Sixty-seven-year-old Salem Assaf specialized in lunch meats for 27 years.

Enterprising Angelo Amato opened this sidewalk fruit stand within 48 hours of the Central Market fire. *(Cleveland State University, Cleveland* Press *Collection)*

Sixty-five-year-old Arthur C. Russ amassed 38 years experience selling spring lamb. At age 54, E. A. McArthur had already accumulated 40 years specializing in mutton. Emma Noss sold cookies for 25 years after her parents operated the same stand for 39 years. Fred Rehfuss peddled pork for 35 years.

The Cleveland *Press*, expressing empathy for the merchants whose livelihoods had been destroyed, commented, "Perhaps it is not too much to hope that, in the long run, they may benefit from the fire as much as all Greater Cleveland is sure to." With little delay, the resolute merchants transformed the hopeful Cleveland *Press* dream into a stunning reality. Angelo Amato, an 18-year market veteran, launched the comeback efforts by creating a makeshift fruit stand at Broadway and Woodland avenues within 48 hours of the blaze, even as heaps of rubble smoked in the background.

Politicians suggested erecting a large tent to temporarily house a makeshift market. Another option involved using short-term space in a newly paved parking lot across from the West Side Market. The venerable market tenants quickly developed a more practical, longer-lasting alternative by leasing space in the nearby building once housing the Sheriff Street Market. Within a few days of the fire, the vendors negotiated a ten-year lease on 27,000 square feet of selling space on the main floor. Four tenants assumed officers' positions in the privately held New Central Market Corporation:

Kenneth Pickering (President), a beef dealer, worked in the market as a child, helping his father who founded the business in 1891. Carrying on the family tradition, he sold beef with the assistance of his wife and 16-year-old son.

Harry Doering (Vice President), a tenant since 1919, operated a butter stand with his brother Harry, as they continued the business founded by their father.

John Catalano (Secretary), a grocer, had been with the Central Market for only five years. He specialized in bulk beans, rice, and ground-to-order poppy seed. Catalano opened the market's first self-serve grocery department.

Calvin Weimer (Treasurer), a pork seller for 11 years, purchased live pigs, had the animals slaughtered in the west side stock yards, and then performed all the butchering tasks.

The New Central Market opened about three months after the devastating Central Market fire.

The Sheriff Street Market (1891 - 1936)

The privately owned Sheriff Street Market, located just one block north of the Central Market, created a fiercely competitive environment by providing modern conveniences for tenants and an aesthetically pleasing environment for shoppers. A great central iron and glass dome, flanked by two cold-storage towers, highlighted the impressive architectural design. Five lengthy main aisles contained 312 stands used by about 100 vendors. Since each stand connected to individual cold air conduits beneath the floor, produce and meat remained fresh. The new facility absorbed Fourth Street's entire 400-foot frontage between Huron and Bolivar roads, extending 123 feet on Huron and 128 feet on Bolivar.

On opening day, 183 ground-floor stands serviced the public while

construction continued on an upper level. Shoppers compared quality and prices among 88 butcher stands selling beef, pork, lamb, turkeys, ducks, geese, and chickens. Shoppers selected from an array of distinctive sausages, each patterned after flavors originating in Hungary, Germany, Italy, Poland, and other countries.

Customers visited 31 stands offering butter and cream products, 13 stands specializing in teas, five stands offering candy, and four stands selling flowers. The Garden Park Greenhouse created a tempting bargain by pricing cut roses at 35 cents per dozen. The remaining 42 stands

carried produce, a variety of fish along with live eels and turtles, cheese ranging from limburger to skim-milk, as well as home-made pickles, jelly, and mincemeat made from pig's heads.

In 1900, the Brandt Provision charged ten cents for a basket of good peaches and 20 cents for a "double-A quality" basket. A large head of cabbage sold for three cents; boneless rolled roast beef, a hind quarter of lamb, or sirloin steak all sold for ten cents per pound. The Cleveland Pure Milk Company cautioned "selling adulterated milk is not as bad as selling diseased milk." The company did all its own pasteurization, while the "other fellow" might not.

In 1900, the modern Sheriff Street Market contained 312 market stands used by about 150 vendors. *(Cleveland Public Library, Photographic Collection)*

Customers and merchants interact at the Sheriff Street Market in 1928. *(Cleveland Public Library, Photographic Collection)*

Sheriff Street customers examine food offerings in 1930. The following week, a serious fire destroyed a major portion of the market. *(Cleveland Public Library, Photographic Collection)*

FROM A MARKET STAND TO AN INTERNET SITE

Customers throughout the world consult the web site of Hirt's Flowers when in need of Venus fly traps, Arabian tea jasmine plants, yellow Christmas cactuses, flowering onion bulbs, or other exotic flowers and plants. Today's internet-based technology would have seemed incomprehensible to Samuel Hirt, the company's founder. At the age of 14, orphan Samuel worked his way from Austria to America on an ocean freighter. In 1915, Hirt founded his company by raising vegetables and selling the harvest, along with horseradish, at a Sheriff's Street Market stand.

Customers and merchants interact at the Sheriff Street Market in 1928. *(Cleveland Public Library, Photographic Collection)*

New Market House, Cleveland, Ohio.

Two cold-storage towers framed the northern and southern boundaries of the Sheriff Street Market which opened on December 24, 1891. *(Alan Dutka collection)*

The 20th Century ushered in a substantially tougher competitive climate for market dealers. In 1901, the Great Atlantic and Pacific Tea Company opened a Central Market store; a Sheriff Street Market venture followed the next year. The A&P stores offered a large variety of food and household items including prunes (35 to a pound priced at three pounds for 25 cents), baked beans (eight cents per can), tomato ketchup (two-pint decanters for 25 cents), a pound of creamery butter (25 cents), starch (four cents per pound or 25 cents for seven pounds), and laundry soap (seven cakes for 25 cents). Market vendors, however, successfully overcame A&P's challenge because shoppers valued the personal service and past history of quality offered by individual sellers. Both market-based A&P stores closed in 1905.

A 1919 scandal propelled the Sheriff Street Market into the national spotlight. The government accused users of the market's cold storage facilities of hoarding hundreds of pounds of beef, poultry, pork, rabbits, and other meat, sometimes for as long as three years, to capitalize on rapidly increasing food prices during World War I. Although the market itself did not engage in illegal behavior, the investigation found two prominent wholesalers guilty of violating cold storage laws; the Cleveland Provision Company and the Cleveland branch of Swift Meat each paid the maximum $500 penalty plus costs.

A MODEST CREAMERY MATURES INTO A CORPORATE COLOSSUS

Abraham Stouffer and his father James founded the Medina County Creamery, operating in the Sheriff Street Market from 1906 to 1920. In 1916, the creamery sold fresh farm eggs (44 cents per dozen), fresh cottage cheese (10 cents per pound), butter (38 cents per pound) and a full line of foreign and domestic cheeses.

In 1922, Abraham and his wife Nahala opened a dairy stand in the Old Arcade, offering buttermilk, toasted cheese sandwiches, homemade deep-dish Dutch apple pie, freshly brewed coffee, and free crackers. Their son Vernon joined the company the following year after his graduation from the Wharton School of Finance. In 1924, the family opened a lunch operation in the Citizens Building at the corner of Euclid Avenue and East Ninth Street, featuring four sandwiches priced from 20 to 25 cents. The company expanded to Detroit and Pittsburgh while a younger son, Gordon, joined the business. By 1936, the restaurant venture had grown to 10 locations.

In 1946, Stouffer's opened its first suburban-styled restaurant on Cleveland's Shaker Square. Paving the way for the ubiquitous TV dinners, Shaker Square customers requested frozen versions of their favorite menu items to reheat at home. The highly successful effort resulted in the company renaming itself Stouffer Foods Corporation in 1954. From its beginnings at the Sheriff Street Market, the Stouffer family expanded the business into one of the country's best known brand names for frozen food products. Litton Industries purchased the company in 1967 and sold it to Nestle in 1973. Stouffer's headquarters is still located in Northeast Ohio.

Edward L. Benedict and his son Edward Scott Benedict operated a creamery in the Sheriff Street Market from 1911 to 1929. Prices between 1916 and 1919 illustrate the escalating cost of food during the First World War. One pound of New York State Cheese rose from 20 cents to 38 cents; one dozen fresh farm eggs increased from 44 cents to 59 cents. *(Alan Dutka collection)*

Benedict's Creamery, 2235 East 4th St., Cleveland, Ohio.

On May 9, 1930, fire destroyed much of the market, including a portion being converted into a bus terminal. First reports of the fire did not surface until 2:00 a.m. Firefighters relied on 14 policemen to restrain a large crowd of gawkers; the curious spectators included many fashionably dressed opera patrons who had attended a Metropolitan Opera presentation of Rimsky-Korsakov's *Sadko* at Public Hall a few hours before the blaze started.

George A. Wallace, Cleveland's legendary 82-year-old fire chief, personally commanded the challenging firefighting effort. Water failed to penetrate the airtight windows of the north storage tower, and the unrestrained flames roared 75 feet into the air above Fourth Street and Huron Road. Eight firefighters temporarily succumbed to treacherous ammonia fumes, a compound most likely used as a refrigerant in the cold storage towers. The inferno transformed the market into a heap of twisted steel and hot bricks, emitting an eerie orange-red glow over downtown Cleveland. Only the market's south section survived the mammoth blaze.

A parking lot replaced the wreckage once comprising the market's primary selling space; and fewer than 30 merchants remained in the still-functional southern portion. In 1931, these resilient vendors unsuccessfully attempted to boost revenue by offering Merchant's Red Stamps, a competitor to the popular Eagle Stamps. The market's customer base, severely weakened by the fire, continued its unrelenting decline, leaving only 12 lingering vendors in 1936.

Not including the suburbs, Cleveland's neighborhoods now supported 2,145 grocery stores, including 245 Fisher Brothers locations, along with numerous dairies and butcher shops which seemed to materialize within a few blocks of every home in the city. The rival Central Market, a decayed old structure still attracting thousands of customers each week, remained in the next block. The once-stunning Sheriff Street Market, much too small to generate a consistent profit, closed after serving Cleveland for 45 years. Downtown Chevrolet, replacing meat and produce with steel, glass, and rubber, leased the building's main floor for automobile storage.

The New Central Market (1950 - 1988)

The New Central Market's opening reunited customers from the burned-out Central Market with veteran merchants Ed Hancy (age 73), C. W. McDonnell (age 70), John C. Koenigshoff (age 69),

The New Central Market, occupying a portion of the former Sheriff Street Market, is now the site of the Quicken Loans Arena. *(Cleveland State University, Cleveland Press Collection)*

Ben Whitmore (age 67), and Arthur Russ (age 65). In fact, only 40 of the old Central Market's tenants failed to relocate to the sparkling new facility. These 168 merchants welcomed three new tenants, Abe Macron, George Fedor, and Moe Nahas, all of whom had already established loyal followings in Cleveland. Macron, a downtown florist since 1907, sold cut flowers and growing plants, whereas Fedor had dealt in bulk spices on Ontario Street for 20 years. Nahas created a 24-seat market restaurant, remembered for its distinctive horseshoe-shaped counter. He also continued to operate Moe's Main Street, a club located on Euclid Avenue at East 77th Street. The Main Street nightspot helped launch the careers of Johnnie Ray, Tony Bennett, the Four Aces, Four Freshmen, and Four Lads, also earning distinction as the site where Bennett met his first wife.

Newspaper advertising hyped the market as "bright, clean, the finest market in Cleveland." The new facility promised "80 carloads of fresh produce arriving each day" and "delicacies arriving by train, boat, truck and air." Radio airwaves emitted the market's infectious jingle:

New Central Market where it's
 fun to shop
New Central Market where
 quality is top
You do your shopping the
 one-stop way
A thousand different items,
 everything is on display
New Central Market where
 the prices are low
New Central Market, the place
 you want to go.

Even from its opening day, the New Central Market faced virtually insurmountable odds in its quest to remain a profitable private enterprise. The city-owned and subsidized West Side Market, a formidable competitor, offered ample free parking as an added inducement. Large chain stores and smaller "mom and pop" businesses followed the inexorable flight to the outskirts of the city and into the suburbs. Convenience stores, cropping up throughout the area, delivered the downtown market another severe blow. The Akron-based Lawson Company's rousing "Roll On, Big O" television commercial relegated the market's radio jingle to a stodgy, blasé status. The visually inspiring advertisement depicted an enormous Lawson tank truck hurriedly rolling across America's newly built freeways, stopping neither day nor night, to transport fresh Florida orange juice to Clevelanders in only 40 hours:

Roll On, Big O
Get that juice up to Lawson's
   in 40 hours
Now the oranges ripen in the
   Florida sun
Sweet on the tree they stay
Then they pick 'em and they squeeze
Just as quick as you please
And the Big O leaves the same day.
Roll On, Big O

Get that juice up to Lawson's
   in 40 hours
Now one man sleeps while the other
   man drives
On the nonstop Lawson's run
And the cold, cold juice
In the tank truck caboose
Stays as fresh as the Florida sun
Roll On, Big O
Get that juice up to Lawson's
   in 40 hours.

The opening of a full-service downtown grocery store in the 1970s contributed another jolt to the market's business. By 1981, the New Central Market served only 25,000 customers per month, and the 40 remaining tenants paid $600 per month in rent for an 18-foot counter and cooler space. The struggling market closed completely in 1988, making way for the glittering Gateway sports complex. Presently, between three and four million people flock to the former Central Market and Sheriff Street Market sites each year to witness events at Progressive Field and the Quicken Loans Arena.

More than 30 years after its opening, the New Central Market still looked inviting in 1981. Unfortunately, rent increases and a declining customer base threatened the economic vitality of the market.
(Cleveland State University, Cleveland Press Collection)

Chapter IV
Dime Store Alley

TIMELINE

1912	F. W. Woolworth's new variety store on Euclid Avenue contained a side entrance on the west side of Fourth Street.
1923	S. S. Kresge constructed its largest U. S. store on the former Opera House site.
1924	J. G. McCrory opened it first variety store in Cleveland on Euclid Avenue with an entrance on the east side of Fourth Street.
1950	A new Euclid Avenue Woolworth store, including a new Fourth Street entrance, replaced the store constructed in 1912.
1954	The McCrory store closed.
1966	The landmark Kresge store closed.
1997	Woolworth closed the Euclid Avenue store along with all its other U. S. stores.

Euclid Avenue's glory days usually invoke images of magnificent department stores and exclusive clothing shops, yet these lofty recollections completely overlook the street's south side between Public Square and the Euclid Arcade. Within that six-block expanse, shoppers delighted at an amazing assortment of nearly side-by-side bargain and five-and-dime palaces.

The shopping paradise, appealing to lunch-counter devotees and purchasers of modestly priced merchandise, began at Public Square with a S. S. Kresge located within the May Company Building. Following in rapid succession, shoppers encountered national retailers W. T. Grant, F. W. Woolworth, S. S. Kresge (a second time), and J. G. McCrory. When physically possible, architectural designs included an obligatory side entrance facing Fourth Street. If the Euclid Avenue segment exemplified the boulevard of bargain shopping, then Fourth Street deserved recognition as the reigning alley of five-and-dimes.

326 Euclid Avenue: F. M. Kirby (1897 - 1908)

Fred Morgan Kirby, born in 1861, attended school until the age of 14 when he obtained his first job as an errand boy in a dry goods store. Kirby, along with Charles Sumner Woolworth, brother of the much more illustrious Frank Woolworth, combined their meager accumulated earnings of about $300 to establish a five-and-ten-cent store in Wilkes-Barre, Pennsylvania. In 1887, barely three years into their newfound partnership, Kirby purchased Woolworth's complete interest in the firm, both founding brand new companies. The long-forgotten F. M. Kirby Company, the pioneering establishment that launched downtown Cleveland's dime store row, opened its Euclid Avenue store in 1897. Gutted by a spectacular fire, the Kirby store operated for only 12 years.

The Kirby dime store and the M. Philipsborn men's clothing shop shared first-floor space in the Rust and Backus Building, located on Euclid Avenue just west of Fourth Street. At 10:40 a.m., on the bitterly cold Sunday morning of November 15, 1908, Harry Janson diligently performed his window dressing duties at the Philipsborn store, creating a sparkling new display for Monday morning shoppers. No one but Janson ever witnessed the results of his labors. Observing smoke pouring from the upper floors, Janson dashed to the fourth floor, verified the fire's origin, and then,

demonstrating even greater zeal, rushed from the burning building.

The treacherous fire vividly illustrated the ever-present dangers tormenting firefighters at the time. As ten firemen entered the building's precarious fourth floor, flames swooped down an elevator shaft, and destroying wooden stairs between the second and third floors, eliminated the only route to safety. One by one, firemen jumped from a third-floor window, the blinding smoke obliterating any view of their ultimate landing point. As Lieutenant Albert Kaercher leaped, he struck the edge of a skylight before landing. The accident crushed his chest, broke three ribs, and dislocated his wrist. Meanwhile, on the second floor, melted pipes discharged dangerous gas into the heart of the blaze, while a five-story, 16-inch wall between the Kirby and Philipsborn stores collapsed. Part of the water intended to quench the perilous fire landed on the heads and faces of firefighters. As the frigidly cold day progressed, icicles formed on their helmets, rubber coats, and mustaches, amusing thousands of on-lookers searching for inexpensive Sunday

Cleveland firefighters employ their tall fire tower, a device used to combat blazes in the city's growing number of skyscrapers that often reached eight stories, to drench the Kirby building with water at the rate of 1,000 gallons per minute. The building, originally housing the Brainard music empire, burned to the ground on November 15, 1908. *(Alan Dutka collection)*

afternoon and evening entertainment.

Following the ruinous fire, the owner of the building announced, "Work of reconstruction will begin as soon as the bricks are cold." The new building, constructed in 1909, is now part of the Fourth Street Windsor Block. In 1912, Fred Kirby merged his 96-store chain with F. W. Woolworth, assuming a vice president position in the Woolworth Corporation.

330 Euclid Avenue and 2020 East Fourth Street: F. W. Woolworth (1912 -1950)

Frank Winfield Woolworth's initial five-cent emporium, an 1879 retailing experiment in Utica, New York, failed within one year. His successful second attempt, in Lancaster, Pennsylvania, established the momentum to launch Woolworth's international retailing empire. In 1912, the growing chain merged with five other retailers, including a chain owned by his brother Charles, to acquire a powerful nationwide presence with 596 locations. The F. M Kirby five-and-dime at 330 Euclid Avenue would have been one of the outlets acquired in Woolworth's expansion had it not already burned to the ground. Woolworth constructed a larger store in about the same location, prominently fronting Euclid Avenue, sharply wrapping around the corner of Fourth Street, and continuing down the narrow block, its

In the early 1930s, the original Woolworth store occupied the southwest corner of Euclid Avenue and Fourth Street; the neighboring southeast corner housed a Kresge location. The J. G. McCrory Company operated a variety store directly east of the Kresge site; W. T. Grant soon joined the bargain retailers, building an outlet west of Woolworth's. With another Kresge's on Public Square, this six-block section of Euclid Avenue eventually consisted of five large, nearly consecutive, variety stores.
(Cleveland Public Library, Photographic Collection)

The largest Kresge store in the United States fronted both Euclid Avenue and Fourth Street.
(Cleveland Public Library, Photographic Collection)

sturdy wooden floors supporting two levels of merchandising ecstasy.

By 1929, Woolworth dominated five-and-ten-cent retailing in the U.S.; its chain of 2,100 outlets dwarfed Kresge's 500 locations and McCrory's 220 stores. Woolworth's merchandise escalated above the ten-cent barrier when the company dropped its nickel and dime price limits in 1935. As prices continued relentlessly upward, the five-and-dimes eventually renamed themselves variety stores. In 1950, Woolworth relocated its Euclid Avenue site just west of the original

location. The Euclid Avenue portion of the initial site, used as a temporary exhibition center in 2010, is a planned location for Cleveland's downtown visitor center. The House of Blues restaurant occupies the former Fourth Street entrance.

402 Euclid Avenue and 2029 - 2033 East Fourth Street: S. S. Kresge (1923 - 1966)

Sebastian Spering Kresge, a former employee and later partner of James G. McCrory, founded the Kresge Company in 1899. Kresge and McCrorey swapped interests in several jointly owned sites, each creating a competing company. Between 1900 and 1907, the Kresge Company opened stores in eight cities, including an Ontario Street location in Cleveland.

Kresge's launched the four-story Fourth Street outlet with enormous fanfare on January 27, 1923. Prior to the grand opening, the company meticulously chose 200 women for clerk positions from a pool containing more than 2,000 applications. Kresge's took pride in publicizing its exceptionally thorough employment selection process. While experience and competency ranked high as desirable attributes, an assessment of each female's moral character constituted the first hurdle in the vigilant screening procedure. Every potential female employee provided information regarding her church affiliation, age, marital status, and number of children. Exactly how these intriguing demographic variables contributed to the

hiring decision is not precisely known, but past retailing experience entered the employment formula only for candidates judged morally acceptable. The company removed from any future consideration all other aspiring workers.

The Kresge building, designed by Cleveland's famed architectural firm Walker & Weeks, created a two-floor, 26,700-square-foot bargain shopper's delight. The third and fourth floors, originally reserved for Kresge's executive offices, later functioned as merchandise stockrooms. The edifice extended 200 feet down Fourth Street and 60 feet along Euclid Avenue.

Promotional literature portrayed Cleveland's new merchandizing nirvana as Kresge's largest in the U.S. On top of and behind its mahogany counters lay an impressive array of products: dry goods, ready-to-wear clothing, hosiery, muslin underwear, ladies' and children's knitted underwear, infants' wear, handkerchiefs,

By 1935, the Kresge entrance had been set back at an angle to Euclid Avenue; attention-getting display cases replaced part of the old entrance. *(Cleveland Public Library, Photographic Collection)*

Burger King (1979-1989) and Wendy's (1991-2004) later occupied the Kresge site. This picture is from 1988. *(City of Cleveland, Landmarks Commission, Warner Thomas)*

stationery, millinery, ribbons, ladies' neckwear, veilings, jewelry and rings, toilet articles, purses and leather goods, men's and boys' furnishings, notions, toys and games, art goods, records, hardware, house furnishings, player piano rolls, radio equipment, electrical goods, along with a soda fountain and luncheonette. Aside from millinery merchandise, no item cost more than $1.00.

Kresge's promoted the 150-person-capacity soda fountain and luncheonette, located near the site of the old Euclid Avenue Opera House stage, as the largest and most sanitary in Cleveland. Sitting at a handsome counter accented with white marble and expensive tile, shoppers enjoyed economical 25-cent lunches. An especially popular treat consisted of hot dogs covered with steamed, chopped onions.

A lady or gentleman, conveniently stationed at a Kresge piano, played

customers' potential sheet music selections to ensure buyers thoroughly enjoyed their picks before making a purchase. A singer, using a piece of sheet music as an improvised megaphone, sometimes accompanied the piano player. Piano rolls of popular instrumentals sold for 30 cents; currently popular vocal selections commanded 50 cents since the piano rolls also contained printed lyrics. Phonograph records, selling for 35 cents, featured the popular hits "He May Be Your Man but He Comes to See Me Sometimes," "Pack Up Your Sins and Go to the Devil," and "Gee but I Hate to Go Home Alone." Patrons engrossed in the new-fangled radio technology purchased the various parts required to assemble a variety of radio receiving sets, including the crystal, miniature tube, and vacuum tube technologies.

An older Kresge site (1911-1984),

situated in the May Company Building, still operated after the opening of the Fourth Street location. The two outlets sold complementary rather than competing, merchandise. Following the inflationary cycle created by World War I, Kresge's created "green-front" stores to sell merchandise priced between 25 cents and $1.00. Among the company's 240 outlets in 1923, 40 carried the "green-front" banner, typified by the Fourth Street location; the remaining 200 stores, including the older May Company Building site, exemplified "red-front" stores featuring items priced at 25 cents or less.

By 1950, the distinction between green and red fronts had faded. Both downtown locations offered identical bargains, including Halo shampoo (25 cents), Pepsodent toothpaste (three sizes selling for 25 cents, 43 cents, and 59 cents), and men's rayon ties with wool lining, bold prints, and pastel shadings (89 cents). In 1962, Kresge's stores featured bowls, cups, and saucers (two for 15 cents), baked ham (99 cents/pound), Baby Ruth and Butterfinger candy bars (three for 10 cents), hot dogs (10 cents), and hot chocolate (five cents).

In 1966, a Jupiter Discount outlet, also owned by the Kresge Company, replaced the old Fourth Street variety store. Jupiter specialized in low-priced, fast-moving merchandise: house wares, drugstore items, clothing, and a limited selection of food. The company typically located the Jupiter brand in deteriorating business areas where unwanted long leases burdened former Kresge outlets. Ironically, when Kresge's opened in 1923, an acre of land at Fourth Street and Euclid Avenue warranted a $5 million tax evaluation – the most valuable parcel in the city of Cleveland.

Today, the Corner Alley resides on the Euclid Avenue portion of the former Kresge store; the Fourth Street Bar and Grill and Pickwick & Frolic occupy the Fourth Street segment. The Cadillac Ranch is the current tenant in Kresge's former location in the May Company Building.

KENNETH CHISHOLM'S 50 YEARS ON FOURTH STREET

C. Kenneth Chisholm's opening of a Fourth Street shoe store is not surprising – his ancestors had pursued merchandising careers for centuries. Chisholm migrated from Canada to Cleveland in 1890, where for six years the 25-year-old obtained employment with the Stone Shoe Company. He then labored for three more years as a traveling salesman with the J. P. Smith Shoe Company. In 1900, Chisholm opened his first store on Superior Avenue. Ten years later, he expanded to Fourth Street at a site later occupied by McCrory's variety store. He moved a few yards north to a storefront in the new Kresge Building when it opened in 1923.

In 1942, Chisholm sold men's brogues for school, street, and dress wear, including lightweight dress oxfords, for $3.85 to $5.65; prices for ladies' Adoree and Beauty Step styles ranged from $2.00 to $4.00. Eight years later, ladies' Naturalizer patent-leather shoes, stocked in an intriguing color selection of red, green, blue, or black, commanded $7.95; children's shoes ranged from $3.95 to $6.45. After 50 years, Chisholm's store closed in 1960. The site continued as a shoe store housing Stevens Shoe City (1961 - 1970) and Michael Stern Shoes (1971 - 1993). The location is currently part of the Pickwick & Frolic complex.

500 - 504 Euclid Avenue and 2041 - 2051 East Fourth Street: J. G. McCrory (1924 - 1954)

John Graham McCrorey opened his first McCrory (he did not use the *e* in the spelling of his stores) location in Scottdale, Pennsylvania, in 1882. Three years later, his chain consisted of five bankrupt Pennsylvania stores. Undaunted, McCrorey started a new and more successful retail business.

The Euclid Avenue/Fourth Street store constituted McCrory's first location in Cleveland. In addition to entrances on Euclid Avenue and Fourth Street, McCrory's customers could also enter from the Euclid Arcade. The variety store contained universal five-and-dime merchandise: house wares, shoes, clothes, fabrics, candy, toys, and cosmetics. Services included a shoe repair operation where, in 1942, customers paid 44 cents per pair for leather half-soles, sewed while they waited.

The McCrory chain also marketed Oriole Records, a unique label not obtainable in competing dime stores – or anywhere else, for that matter. The records, selling for 25 cents, debuted at McCrory's in 1921. The label marketed competent cover versions of current trendy songs, typified by the 1931 hit "I Found a Million Dollar Baby (in a Five and Ten Cent Store)." In addition to creating a superb anthem for dime stores, the song soared in popularity with three artists recording major hit versions: Fred Waring's Pennsylvanians, Bing Crosby, and the Boswell Sisters. Oriole needed only 20 days to cover the Crosby recording, even using the identical song on the flip side. The Oriole recording featured talented Chick Bullock, a skilled studio musician for Duke Ellington; Cab Calloway; Tommy

Dorsey; Jimmy Dorsey, and numerous other major artists. Although he recorded about 500 songs, Bullock never attained mainstream star status. A disfigured face, caused by an eye disease, prevented his performing in front of audiences. Bullock epitomized the profile for an Oriole cover artist: a talented performer, who, for whatever reason, never captured the musical limelight. The Oriole label stopped production in 1937, doomed by the Great Depression, the popularity of radio, and the difficult-to-imitate sounds of the emerging dance bands.

After 30 years, McCrory's closed the Fourth Street site in 1954. In 1992, the McCrory chain declared bankruptcy and switched many of its locations to a "dollar store" format. The conversions failed to salvage the company. McCrory's entered bankruptcy again in 2001, this second dose of insolvency ending the company's existence. On Fourth Street, Lynn's Clothing occupied the street-level portion for 28 years, and several beauty academies operated on the second floor for 47 years. The Fourth Street frontage is currently under construction for the planned Dredgers Union retail store; the Euclid Avenue site is now part of the Corner Alley.

306-318 Euclid Avenue and 2046 - 2050 East Fourth Street: F. W. Woolworth (1950 - 1997)

The second Woolworth site, dazzling entire families with two floors of moderately priced merchandise, premiered on August 14, 1950. Delighted women seized pairs of "hep cat sloppy-floppy" socks (39 cents), cover-girl blouses ($1.00), three pairs of whisper-shear nylons ($2.59), and a Toni spin curler combination including the refill ($2.29). Pragmatic men purchased serviceable gray work pants ($2.45),

Two venerable bank buildings flank Stone's shoe store on Euclid Avenue, just west of East Fourth Street. The first Euclid Avenue Woolworth store is to the left. To the right, the Union Trust building (occupied by the Brotherhood of Locomotive Engineer's Bank at the time of this picture) along with the Stone Shoe building, will be razed to make room for Woolworth's new downtown store. Lerner, Petrie, and City Blue clothing stores later occupied the ground floor of the former Euclid Building (left). Now part of Fourth Street's Windsor Block, the Euclid Building (at the time of this photo home to the State Banking and Trust Company) incurred a radical change created by the removal of its upper tower in 1926. *(Cleveland State University, Bruce Young Collection)*

The new F. W. Woolworth Company store brought a modern look to lower Euclid Avenue. The store also had an entrance from East Fourth Street. The W. T. Grant variety store is directly west of the Woolworth building. *(Cleveland State University, Bruce Young Collection)*

blue work shirts ($1.19), and two Gillette razor blades for a dime. Overjoyed children snapped up 28-inch dolls with washable latex arms and legs ($9.98), four-unit electric trains ($4.95), and a Texas gun shooting real smoke (98 cents). Not forgetting the faithful family pet, Woolworth's offered half-inch leather dog harnesses (29 cents).

A 69-cent investment garnered a popular, classical, spiritual, polka, or children's record in the newer, increasingly popular 45 rpm vinyl technology. Both accomplished and would-be athletes acquired archery sets ($2.98 to $5.98), boxing gloves ($1.98 to $3.79), and tennis rackets ($4.98 to $8.98). Bicycles for adults and children ranged from $7.98 to $31.50. Thoroughly practical-minded shoppers obtained Cannon towels (three for $1.00), Dial deodorant soap (19 cents) and Black & Decker electric drills ($18.95). A bakery tempted customers with tasty coconut macaroons (49 cents/pound) and scrumptious iced, raised, or glazed doughnuts (48 cents/dozen).

Woolworth's crammed 157 stools along a 300-foot lunch counter, leaving each hungry shopper with about 23 inches of his or her own private eating space. Customers eagerly devoured dinners comprised of turkey (60 cents), Swiss steak (60 cents), meatloaf (50 cents) and vegetables (40 cents), along with pieces of layer cake (10 cents), apple or cherry pies (15 cents), peach tulip sundaes (20 cents), and squeezed-fresh orange juice (10 cents).

Woolworth's moderately priced merchandise provided many young shoppers with their first opportunity to make purchases without parental supervision. One such experience remained firmly etched in a shopper's mind, even after the passage of nearly 60 years. Back in 1952, two fifth-grade schoolgirls completed their first downtown outing without a chaperoning parent. One of the ten-year-olds paid $2.95 to obtain a glass pitcher and six matching glasses, each with hand-painted flowers, for her mother's Christmas present. She also recalled mom's ensuing lecture about spending too much money for the gift. A decade later, a teenaged student at the Ohio Beauty College, directly across from Woolworth's, recalled her 1960s lunch trips to the dime store, usually

Shoppers investigate a world of new bargains at Woolworth's on opening day, August 14, 1950. *(Cleveland State University, Cleveland Press Collection)*

including a BLT sandwich and milkshake, followed by hurried journeys to the store's makeup and nail polish department. Using money obtained from her beauty college customers' tips, she gained her first experiences in becoming a self-sufficient shopper without her parent's supervision. The dime stores also offered employment opportunities for teenagers, further cultivating independence and lessons in money management.

In the 1970s, an exciting selection of pinball machines occupied a space to the right of the Fourth Street entrance. With the arrival of the video age, Pac-Man and Space Invaders rendered pinball machines passé. A men's clothing department highlighting socks, underwear, and T-shirts replaced the pinball corner.

In 1962, Woolworth's and Kresge's implemented a dramatic change in strategic direction, ushering in the end of the variety store era. Both companies expanded their merchandise selection to compete directly with large, full-line department stores. Woolworth launched Woolco outlets and Kresge countered with Kmart centers. Woolco stores graced the country's landscape for only one generation. Unable to compete with Kmart, all 336 U.S. Woolco locations closed in 1982. In 1987, Kmart sold all of its remaining Kresge and Jupiter stores in the U.S. to the McCrory's chain. Kmart filed for Chapter 11 bankruptcy protection in 2002, merging with Sears two years later. Although unappreciated at the time, Woolworth's implemented a dramatically important long-term decision when the Kinney Shoe Division created the Foot Locker chain in 1974.

The old variety stores declined rapidly in the 1980s and 1990s, but the Fourth Street Woolworth's still found a way to generate a few lasting memories. A 30-something professional recalled

his boring childhood shopping trips to the Fourth Street clothing stores with his grandmother. If he demonstrated good behavior during these ordeals, his final destination consisted of a journey to Woolworth's basement to select one of the many inexpensive but appealing toys. Hurrying past a pet department displaying whistling parakeets, lively kittens, and gnawing hamsters, he reached the toy department where his gallant patience during grandmother's shopping jaunts eventually created a noteworthy collection of GI Joe figures, Teenage Mutant Ninja Turtle characters, and plastic gotcha guns.

In 1997, Woolworth shuttered its remaining 400 U.S. outlets, including the Euclid Avenue/Fourth Street location. Four years later, the corporate name changed to Foot Locker, the Woolworth name vanishing after more than a century as a retailing icon. Presently, the House of Blues concert hall occupies the Euclid Avenue segment of the former Woolworth store; the Fourth Street entrance is now La Strada restaurant.

Manager O. W. Shannon and employee Mrs. Besse Lorenz pose in front of the Woolworth Christmas corsage display in 1964. *(Cleveland State University, Cleveland Press Collection)*

Chapter V
Urban Pioneers

TIMELINE

1982	Merchants established the East Fourth Street Local Development Corporation.
1985	Fourth Street became a Cleveland Landmark District.
1986	Fourth Street achieved status as a National Register of Historic Places District.
1994	A new baseball park and arena launched redevelopment efforts on nearby Fourth Street.
1996	The formerly dilapidated Buckeye Building reopened as upscale apartments.
1997	Flannery's Irish Pub, the first of the new wave of Fourth Street restaurants, opened in the Buckeye Building.
1997	The Windsor Block reopened as the second Fourth Street apartment building.
2002	The Pickwick & Frolic entertainment complex opened.
2004	The House of Blues established a concert hall (Euclid Avenue) and restaurant (Fourth Street).
2006	The upscale Corner Alley bowling alley and restaurant opened.
2007	The Gateway Church conducted its first worship service.

The creation of Fourth Street's 21st Century urban lifestyle and entertainment center required 20 years of concerted effort, unfolding in four interrelated yet distinct stages: (a) a grassroots organization to place Fourth Street in the National Register of Historic Places, thus ensuring the preservation of the buildings, (b) innovative public/private cooperation to generate the funds necessary to revive the tired and neglected street, (c) the creation of an extraordinary vision to rebuild Fourth Street, and (d) the recruitment of pioneering entertainment venues to demonstrate the economic viability required to attract additional establishments. In each of these stages, individuals emerged with different and sometimes conflicting agendas, but each shared a passion to restore Fourth Street to its 19th Century position as a center for entertainment and dining.

Stage One:
The Grass Roots Organization

In 1996, the Cleveland Restoration Society presented the proprietor of the Sisser jewelry store on Fourth Street with a certificate containing an intriguing inscription: "When the history of East Fourth Street is written, the spirit of Bob Zimmer will be felt on every page." Without Zimmer's vision, determination, and organizational efforts, the vibrant Fourth Street of the 21st Century might

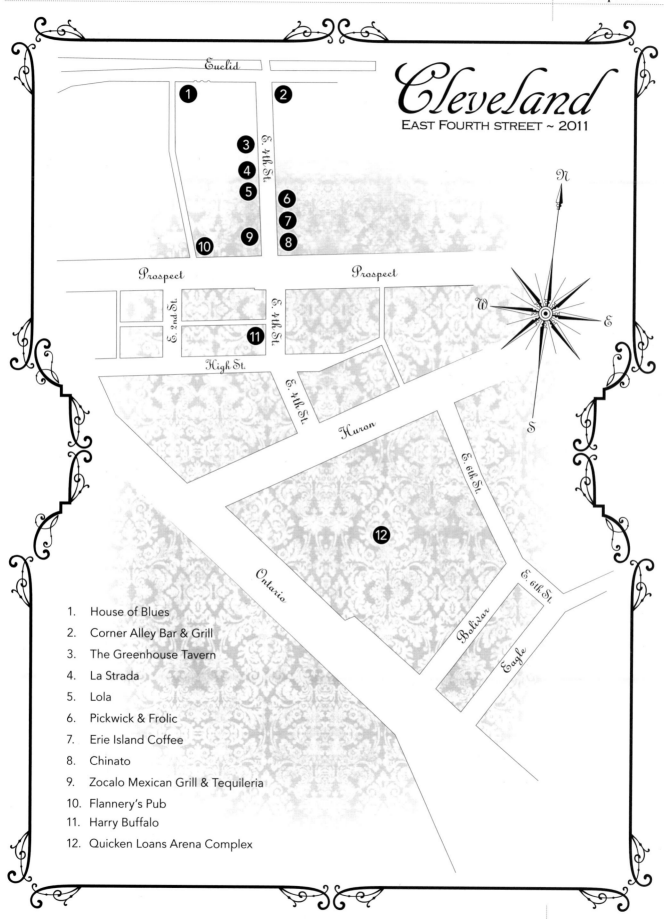

Cleveland
EAST FOURTH STREET ~ 2011

1. House of Blues
2. Corner Alley Bar & Grill
3. The Greenhouse Tavern
4. La Strada
5. Lola
6. Pickwick & Frolic
7. Erie Island Coffee
8. Chinato
9. Zocalo Mexican Grill & Tequileria
10. Flannery's Pub
11. Harry Buffalo
12. Quicken Loans Arena Complex

Fourth Street merchants, offering support to the Cleveland Indians, pose at the street's intersection with Prospect Avenue. Bob Zimmer is the far right merchant in this 1989 photograph autographed to Sam and Ben, Zimmer's children, by Jesse Orosco, a Cleveland Indian relief pitcher from 1989 through 1991. Orosco made his major league pitching debut on April 5, 1979, and his last outing on September 27, 2003.
(Robert Zimmer)

not physically exist; construction of the Gateway sports complex obliterated many of the nearby streets, and Fourth Street could have easily been one of the fatalities.

Abraham Sisser founded a jewelry store in the Buckeye Building on Fourth Street in 1911. The landmark business survived two world wars, the Great Depression, and the massive suburban flight that destroyed most of downtown Cleveland's once enormous retail presence. Sisser's brother-in-law later purchased the business, selling it in the 1950s to Irving Zimmer, a former employee of the nearby Volk Jewelers. With quality comparable to Rodgers Jewelers, a competitor located in the same building, Irving developed a loyal market niche by extending credit, payment plans, and layaways to lower income but trusted customers, most of whom could not obtain comparable terms elsewhere.

Bob Zimmer received an early indoctrination into the jewelry business when, at the age of six, he began helping his father polish rings and clean merchandise. Growing up with the business, Bob worked in sales while performing many other essential tasks. In the 1970s, he founded Green Mansions, an art and antique gallery in the Shaker Square neighborhood. Bob returned downtown to manage Sisser Jewelers in 1979, although his father still owned the business. In 1997, after conversion of the Buckeye Building to apartments, Bob relocated the store to the Krause Building where the business remained until its closing in 2003.

As the street declined in the 1980s, Zimmer founded the East Fourth Street Local Development Corporation to combat a growing public perception of crime, drugs, and prostitution within the immediate neighborhood. The development group sponsored festivals, artist receptions and displays, sports promotions, and other activities to encourage shopping on Fourth Street. These marketing efforts became the forerunner to the influential Historic Gateway Neighborhood Corporation. Zimmer served as first president of both organizations.

Almost concurrently, City leaders immersed themselves in planning the mammoth downtown Gateway project, a multi-million dollar undertaking culminating in a gleaming new baseball park and equally impressive sports arena. As their planning began in earnest, some movers and shakers proposed razing every building on the then-forlorn Fourth Street, leaving a vast wasteland suitable for immediate parking lots and future undetermined development. In fact, demolition of scores of seedy-looking buildings framing the southern portion of downtown Cleveland developed into a major

selling point in promoting the costly project to wary taxpayers. The razing of Fourth Street's decaying old buildings fit perfectly into the revitalization master plan.

Bob Zimmer spearheaded efforts to specify Fourth Street between Euclid and Prospect avenues a Cleveland Landmark District (1985) and a National Register of Historic Places District (1986); these designations sheltered the street from destruction by unforgiving wrecking balls. Ironically, the Cleveland Landmark District proposal contained this advice: "East Fourth Street should not become urban 'chic.' Rather, it should remain a diverse, pedestrian part of downtown."

Zimmer's triumph in saving Fourth Street met with less than enthusiastic acceptance by some members of the business community and downright hostility from a few building owners who welcomed demolition of their properties. A president of a major Cleveland bank, calling for the "clean up" of Fourth Street, left little doubt that "clean

On July 28, 1992, Cleveland Mayor Michael R. White (left) and Councilman Gus Frangos (right) join nine-year-old Sam Zimmer as he cuts a ribbon dedicating a storefront renovation in the Historic Gateway Neighborhood. At the ceremony, Bob Zimmer chose his son to signify the future in his philosophy of remembering the past, taking action in the present, and preparing for the future. At the time, Bob hoped his children would grow up to witness a flourishing downtown with Fourth Street comprising part of an energetic neighborhood.
(Plain Dealer, Chris Stephens)

up" and annihilation could be used synonymously. Next, Zimmer actively directed development of three critical Fourth Street planning projects involving urban design guidelines (1989), a planning and development strategy (1992), and a financial feasibility analysis for housing (1995). These efforts supplied the structure and rigor needed to keep alive the dream of Fourth Street's revitalization.

Zimmer, appreciating downtown's potential as a legitimate city neighborhood, functioned as a storekeeper, grassroots organizer, marketer, and visionary. For these gallant efforts, Zimmer received the Cleveland Restoration Society's award for "Creative and Effective Preservation Advocacy of the East Fourth Street Historic Neighborhood." As Zimmer proudly accepted his laudable award, his jewelry store unwittingly entered its final years of existence, an ironically unintended victim of its proprietor's victory in energizing the once drab and decaying downtown street.

Two substantial Fourth Street makeovers within ten years created an aesthetically pleasing new streetscape. But the second renovation consumed far more time than anticipated, disrupting retail activity during two consecutive Christmas seasons by eliminating vehicle traffic and obstructing store entrances. Customers had to walk over piles of dirt and rubble to reach the Sisser store. The street improvement project, however appealing in future years, drained the life from Zimmer's retail jewelry store. A fixture on Fourth Street for 92 years, Sisser Jewelry closed in 2003.

Few customers of Sisser Jewelers challenged the obstacle course created by the Fourth Street improvement project. The store closed after a 92-year run on the street. On rainy evenings, Pickwick & Frolic employees used umbrellas to escort patrons past construction areas to places where valet parkers returned automobiles.
(Megan Krapf)

The Buckeye Building (left) and Sincere Building (right) are Fourth Street anchors on the Prospect Avenue side of the street. Today apartments (Buckeye Building) and condominiums (Sincere Building) are located above street-level restaurants. The photograph is from 1929. *(Rick Parker)*

In 1951 a parade-detoured streetcar turns from Prospect Avenue onto East Second Street. The sign for the Anders Cafeteria in the Buckeye Building is to the right of the scene. Two of Cleveland's favorite bakeries, Kaase's and Rosen's, are also visible in the photo.
(Anthony Krisak collection)

The Anders Cafeteria, a mainstay on the second floor of the Buckeye Building for nearly 40 years, provided food for hungry downtowners from 1923 to 1961. On Fridays in 1942, the cafeteria featured a special 20-cent beef stew, crammed full of potatoes, carrots, peas, and meat. In 1949, a hamburger steak cost 28 cents and a breaded pork chop sold for 35 cents.
(Alan Dutka collection)

Stage Two:
Public/Private Teamwork

Funding Fourth Street's revival incorporated an imaginative mixture of private investment and local, state, and federal assistance. The expertise needed to implement this cooperative effort already existed; the Warehouse District's thriving rejuvenation achieved national recognition by winning a 1997 Rudy Bruner Foundation silver medal for urban excellence. Tom Yablonsky, a pioneer in redeveloping the Warehouse District, assumed a similar leadership role with the Historic Gateway Neighborhood Corporation. In 2001, the two groups merged with Yablonsky serving as head of the combined organization.

Yablonsky, a native of Cleveland's West Park neighborhood, graduated from St. Ignatius High School and earned a bachelor's degree in political science from Cleveland State University and a master's degree in public affairs from Indiana University. Before returning to Cleveland, he acquired essential experience, first as city manager for a small Indiana town, later as a planner in an Indiana agency.

Yablonsky and his staff now perform the often unsung but vitally important behind-the-scenes tasks needed to coordinate government, civic, and business efforts. The staff understands the available incentives and possesses the technical and bureaucratic skills required to maneuver in a sometimes daunting environment. Through Yablonsky's efforts, a myriad of tax deductions, city and state initiatives and civic support are coordinated to fully maximize available tools, including historic preservation tax credits, conservation easements, TIF (Tax Increment Financing), a linked-deposit program, tax abatement, infrastructure improvement, and seed money used for consulting studies and similar activities.

The Federal Historic Preservation Tax Incentives program, encouraging private sector rehabilitation of historic buildings, grants a 20 percent tax credit for historic rehabilitation to buildings either listed individually in the National Register of Historic Places or within a registered historic district. Because of Bob Zimmer's earlier efforts, every building on Fourth Street automatically qualified for this assistance. A more recent State of Ohio Historic Tax Credit initiative assisted the final phase of the Fourth Street apartment conversion.

A conservation easement is a voluntary agreement allowing landowners to limit future development on their property, thus satisfying government land preservation initiatives, while still retaining their private ownership. These easements, binding on all subsequent owners, reduce the future sale price of the land because new owners are restricted in redeveloping the property. The difference in property value, before and after the easement is granted, is the basis for determining the amount of tax deductions. Executions of conservation easements helped finance the redevelopment of the Frederick, Graves, McCrory, and second Woolworth buildings.

TIF (Tax Increment Financing) uses anticipated future tax gains to finance debt needed for current improvements in areas where the enhancements are expected to create increased tax revenue. TIF supports improvement in blighted, distressed, or underdeveloped areas in which development would not otherwise occur. The City of Cleveland declared Fourth Street a TIF district, allowing for the use of tax incremental assistance.

The State of Ohio's linked-deposit program offers borrowers credit at below-market interest rates. The state invests funds in certificates of deposit in Ohio lending institutions, accepting a reduced rate of return. In return, the institution agrees to pass the savings along to borrowers already approved for development loans.

Cleveland also provided infrastructure modernization and tax abatement for residential properties. Civic organizations and foundations supplied seed money for consulting studies and attendance at an ICSC (International Council of Shopping Centers) conference where the networking, education, and deal-making exist to develop and implement a successful redevelopment plan. The City of Cleveland and the Historic Gateway Corporation established BRAG (Blight Remediation Around Gateway), an initiative to remove unsightly security bars and gates placed on Fourth Street storefronts. A design review committee helped enhance the look and feel of the street and assisted in creating alluring signage.

The amount of assistance available to stimulate redevelopment may seem extravagant to some critics, but the urban pioneers receiving this aid also invested large amounts of private funds, including personal savings, in a blighted area that the vast majority of funding sources considered an extremely poor investment risk.

Stage Three: Developing An Urban Neighborhood Vision;

Blighted is a sympathetic depiction of the Buckeye Building's condition in 1995; located on the northwest corner of Fourth Street and Prospect Avenue, this once handsome edifice had surely seen better days. Built in 1906 at a cost of $100,000, the five-story maroon-brick building contains 98 feet of frontage on Fourth Street, initially supporting three retail stores, and 110 feet on Prospect, accommodating another seven retailers. By the 1990s, the Buckeye Building's upper floors, originally designed for light manufacturing, had been vacant for three decades. The street-level storefronts followed a similar progression. The building represented a prime example of urban decay, a seemingly next-to-worthless structure exemplifying the heartbreaking decline of Downtown Cleveland. Adding to this already dismal situation, the rundown structure dominated a high-visibility street corner, continually exposing its decline to thousands of Clevelanders and visitors. Not surprisingly, the City of Cleveland wanted the old eyesore rehabilitated.

Imaginative planners envisioned an urban dweller's delight rising from the dilapidated property. A few widely optimistic visionaries even harbored a fantasy that the building's renovation would spark development of an entire upscale neighborhood. Downtown Cleveland's robust renewal in the mid-1990s provided credibility to the City's inspired vision. In 1994, a state-of-the-art baseball park and sparkling new arena debuted to rave reviews; the Tower City Mall celebrated its fifth anniversary the following year. These pristine entertainment and shopping venues resided within a five-minute walk of the Buckeye Building, as did a daily gathering of thousands of downtown workers and visitors. With the addition of rental property, a few farsighted urban planners viewed a vibrant downtown neighborhood as more inevitable than merely feasible. To test the viability of this optimistic vision, Cleveland leaders chose Richard Maron, founder of MRN Ltd, to rehabilitate the Buckeye Building into fashionable apartments.

The Maron family emigrated from Warsaw to Cleveland in 1922. The parents of brothers Samuel and Aaron possessed only enough money to send one of their two highly intelligent sons to college. The choice would be based strictly on which boy attained the best grades in school. Aaron produced an impressive straight-A record, except for one solitary B in English, his second language. Although Aaron's grades constituted a wonderful achievement, Sam's straight-A grades contained not a single blemish, earning him the coveted college money. Sam made the most of his opportunity, graduating from Western Reserve University, accepting a professorship at Case Institute of Technology, and becoming the driving force in creating the school's Polymer Research Department. His legacy continues as Case Western Reserve University annually honors an undergraduate for excellence in polymer research with the Samuel Maron Memorial Award.

Even without the benefit of a college education, Aaron progressed to a floor manager position at the Sears store on Carnegie Avenue. His son Richard earned a computer science degree and an MBA, both from Ohio State University. After graduation, Richard purchased a tool rental company in Warren from the mother-in-law of his younger brother. He moved back to the Cleveland area, partly because his young son Ari, named after Aaron, the grandfather he never met, attended classes at the Cleveland Institute of Music. Richard founded MRN, a company owning and managing rental properties, primarily in Cleveland Heights, Shaker Heights, and University Heights.

MRN successfully completed the $3.5 million conversion of the Buckeye Building into 36 upscale apartments ranging in size from 465 to 1,800 square feet.

The apartments, opening on March 28, 1996, enjoyed immediate success. Short commutes, combined with the excitement of a growing urban neighborhood, offered a special appeal to young professionals. Television, radio, and newspaper media personnel, most in the early stages of their careers, have gravitated to the building since its opening.

Flannery's Irish Pub, with an attractive décor featuring hardwood floors, mahogany paneling, and brass railings, fills the Buckeye Building's street-level space. Diners enjoy traditional Irish fare including Irish stew and colcannon – a mixture of mashed potatoes, grated cabbage, carrots, scallions, and garlic – along with a selection of American food. The food menu is complemented with an ample selection of beer and Irish whiskies. In 2008, *Irish Voice*, America's largest Irish newspaper, chose Flannery's as one of America's Top 40 Irish pubs and restaurants.

Dennis Flannery, a third-generation Clevelander, previously owned other area pubs including the popular Parnell's Pub, located next to the Cedar-Lee Theater in Cleveland Heights. He met Irish-born John O'Reilly at the Commons Tap (the old Pat Joyce restaurant on Chester Avenue) where John tended bar while studying at John Carroll University on a rugby scholarship. West Virginia native Christine Connell, a third partner, graduated from Ohio University with a degree in political science. She brought with her impressive food service experiences with the Stouffer Restaurant organization, including management responsibilities in Cleveland and New York City.

The pub's regular customers are mostly residents of downtown apartments. But one suburban patron, a Cavaliers, Indians, and Browns season ticket holder, enjoys his own reserved booth near the pub's entrance.

Before St. Patrick's Day crowds begin arriving at five o'clock in the morning, Flannery's furniture has already been removed to accommodate as many patrons as possible with beer, corned beef, and cabbage. The pub is filled to capacity by 9:30 a.m. Revenue for the single day equals or exceeds the otherwise best week in the year, even including the NBA championship or the NCAA Women's Basketball finals.
(Christine Connell)

Flannery's opened in 1997, the year of a Cleveland Indians World Series appearance, Major League Baseball's All-Star game, and the NBA All-Star contest. As Tribe attendance declined in the 21st Century, interest in the Cavaliers increased substantially. In this photograph, Flannery's is inviting Cavs fans to make the pub their 2010 playoff headquarters.
(Christine Connell)

Baseball fans from New York and Boston, some returning each year since the pub opened in 1997, marvel at the inexpensive prices charged by Cleveland's restaurants and hotels. National sportswriters, in town for Gateway events, make Flannery's a repeated stop during their trips; the *Boston Globe's* Dan Shaughnessy, covering the 2010 NBA playoffs, wrote a complimentary article about downtown Cleveland, specifically praising Flannery's.

Irish artists performing in Northeast Ohio frequently find their way to Flannery's after their concerts. Michael Flatley and the entire cast of *Lord of the Dance* celebrated into the early morning hours after their Cleveland appearances. Guests occasionally entertain the Flannery's crowd with an impromptu performance; the Irish rock group Saw Doctors offered *I Useta Lover* while the folk-inspired Irish Rovers sang their old classic about green alligators and long-necked geese.

During the World Cup Playoffs, Clevelanders and travelers from the British Isles enjoy viewing the televised matches in the pub. Prior to British Petroleum's departure from Cleveland, employees on business trips from England often created an atmosphere resembling a British Isles pub. Cultural differences of a serious nature are sometimes apparent. A visitor from terror-weary Dublin once rolled under a parked car on Prospect Avenue after hearing a nearby explosion. Clevelanders paid scant attention to the noise, recognizing it as the familiar sound of fireworks emanating from the baseball scoreboard after a Cleveland Indian home run, this particular occurrence celebrating a blast from the bat of Brian Giles.

Heartened by the Buckeye Building's success, the Marons purchased the Windsor Block, composed of four buildings on the Euclid side of Fourth Street: the Windsor Building (built in 1875), two buildings on Euclid Avenue west of the Windsor Building, (the Rust and Backus (1908) and Lerner (1936) buildings), and the Waverly Building (1875), south of the Windsor Building on Fourth Street. The vintage 1875 Windsor Building, the oldest and most richly decorated Fourth Street structure, contains different-sized windows, a contrasting brick and stone exterior, dark hardwood floors, and exposed brick. Fifty-two apartments, carved from the four buildings and ranging in size from 455 to 1,700 square feet, opened in 1997.

The Marons, now owners of two successful apartment buildings, expected other developers to restore Fourth Street's remaining structures. But the development never materialized, partly because, over the decades, about 250 different people acquired ownership rights in the buildings.

The Windsor Building, part of the Windsor Block renovated by MRN, housed Cleveland's YMCA in the 1880s. The smaller building to the left is the YMCA gymnasium. *(Ralph Horner)*

With an average of nearly 25 owners per structure, the purchase of even one building required considerable research and negotiating efforts. At the time, owners of the Sincere Building paid royalties to 30 different known leaseholders, one receiving $12 per quarter. Seizing an unexpected opportunity, MRN decided to purchase the entire block, allowing the company to control the pace, quality, and composition of the street's renovation. Seven years passed while MRN diligently located owners and bargained with people owning pieces, parts, and slices of the properties. A few out-of-town owners, unaware of their property rights or even cognizant of Fourth Street's location or condition, initially refused to sell their claims. By 2001, MRN's persistence resulted in ownership of about 80 percent of the buildings. A few years later, the company controlled virtually the entire street. About four out of every five owners directly sold their interests, and the remainder entered

into partnerships with MRN. The city threatened a few owners with purchase by eminent domain, but every case concluded with an out-of-court settlement.

Meanwhile Ari Maron continued his lifelong interest in music, earning a bachelor's degree from Rice University where he trained as a classical violinist. Evaluating his alternatives after graduation, Ari speculated his musical talents would take him no further than an orchestra position. He returned to Cleveland expecting to work for his father's company for six months while he formulated his future plans. But recalling the excitement of his childhood visits to downtown Cleveland from Warren, Ari became thoroughly engrossed in the development of Fourth Street. Interest in larger cities waned when Ari realized he could never transform New York or Chicago, but he could change Cleveland. Despite demanding development duties, Ari still enjoys playing in a string quartet and a bluegrass band, along with teaching music to children.

The next phase of Fourth Street's rehabilitation involved converting all of the street's upper floors into apartments. Thirty-six units, debuting in the Commercial Building, featured exposed duct work, huge ceilings, large windows, and mint-green hallways lined with framed art. Next, MRN unveiled 37 apartments in the combined upper floors of the Frederick, McCrory, and Graves buildings. The units are distinctive for their natural wood ceiling beams. The final conversion occurred when 64 apartments opened in the Euclid Block above the Corner Alley; these units contain Jacuzzi tubs and in-suite washers and dryers. In total, Fourth Street now contains 225 apartments. An occupancy rate near 100 percent is typical, and a waiting list for available apartments often exists.

Jori Maron, Ari's younger brother, returned to Cleveland in 2005 after earning a finance and accounting degree from Indiana University, and working for Best Buy Corporation in Minneapolis. Jori now handles the company's accounting, financial modeling, and performance forecasts for potential acquisitions. He also oversees building maintenance, monitoring its quality and efficiency. While Richard is responsible for construction and Ari for negotiating real estate deals, Jori oversees the company's spending. Ari refers to his brother as Oz because money management often involves mysterious number-crunching computer software models, the results often comprehended only by Jori.

Beside the MRN apartments, separate developers converted two Fourth Street buildings into condominiums. The upper floors of the eight-story Sincere Buildings, built in 1913 at a cost of $150,000, now house 12 condominiums originally conceived as live/work space, ranging from 1,800 to nearly 4,000 square feet in size, with separate entrances to accommodate a home and business. The Krause Building is also being converted into condominiums.

Renovation of the Sincere Building involved six months of effort just to clean it and remove the accumulated trash. Without the benefit of modern sophisticated engineering tools, architects overbuilt these buildings to avoid possible structural problems. The majority of Fourth Street's buildings, while in extremely poor physical condition, remained structurally sound and capable of accommodating nearly any type of adaptive reuse. This photograph reflects the condition of the Sincere Building prior to its renovation into condominiums. *(Rick Parker)*

Fourth Street's alluring atmosphere includes inspirations from New York (outdoor dining), Paris (overhead lights), Venice (street design) and Switzerland (bollards not visible in this picture). In this view to the south, the Gateway parking garage is in the background.
(Positivelycleveland, Jeff Greenberg)

While the successful apartment conversions continued, MRN grappled with the challenging question of how to best utilize the street-level storefronts. Fourth Street needed to attract suburbanites, but replicating the stores and amenities already available in the suburbs would not draw people downtown. The Marons developed a much more imaginative approach, creating their urban dreamland by carefully blending distinctive entertainment venues and one-of-a kind dining experiences to complement the trendy apartments. No "site available" or "for lease" signs ever appeared on Fourth Street; instead, the Marons recruited the venues and chefs they deemed the best choices to execute their vision. One restaurant owner considered his invitation from the Marons to be an honor, tantamount to winning an award.

Fourth Street includes multiple entertainment anchor tenants, similar in concept to the department stores supporting suburban retail shopping malls. The Gateway complex, drawing four million people each year and only one block south of Fourth Street, served as a powerful, already existing anchor. The Marons attracted three additional anchors and then created a clustering of unique restaurants offering a wide range of dining choices. In addition to the venues, the distinctive buildings and streetscape contributed to the urban allure.

**Stage Four:
Attracting the Pioneering
Entertainment Venues**

With Flannery's Pub the only Fourth Street restaurant, MRN convinced three pioneering urban anchor establishments (Pickwick & Frolic, the House of Blues, and the Corner Alley) to invest a total of

$22.5 million to convert 94,000 square feet of street-level space into unique entertainment venues. Each success provided additional justification for the continued renovation of the entire block.

Pickwick & Frolic

Brooklyn native Nick Kostis visited Cleveland at the age of 12 to attend the national convention of the Pan-Icarian Brotherhood of America. Founded in 1903 in Pittsburgh, the descendents of the Greek Island Ikaria form the oldest Hellenic organization in the Western Hemisphere. Kostis never forgot his favorable impression of the look and feel of Cleveland's downtown streets. After graduating from high school, Kostis earned a bachelor's degree in secondary education from the University of Rio Grande in Southern Ohio. He selected the school because of its excellent curriculum in education and its close proximity to family members in Huntington, West Virginia. Basketball fanatics still recall Rio Grande as the school for whom, in the 1950s, Bevo Francis personally scored an amazing 116 points against Ashland Junior College of Kentucky and 113 points against Hillsdale College.

The town of Rio Grande, home of the first Bob Evans Restaurant, housed 333 permanent residents when Kostis arrived from Brooklyn. The extraordinary contrasts between his native city and the tiny Ohio community served as a life-changing experience for Kostis; he developed a totally different view of the world, including greater respect for people, an attribute missing from his Brooklyn youth. Without gaining his new perspective, Kostis speculates he might still be hanging around the same Brooklyn pool hall he frequented as a teenager. Kostis has remained an Ohio resident since his college days at Rio Grande in the 1960s.

After graduation, Kostis worked as admissions officer at Rio Grande University, promoting the school to high school students and parents in Ohio, West Virginia, and Pennsylvania. The university's enrollment increased 35 percent during his two-year tenure. He taught high school for one year in West Lafayette, located in Coshocton County. In his next job, he introduced the city of Marietta to counseling methods at the elementary school level.

Earning a master's degree in counseling from Ohio University in 1971,

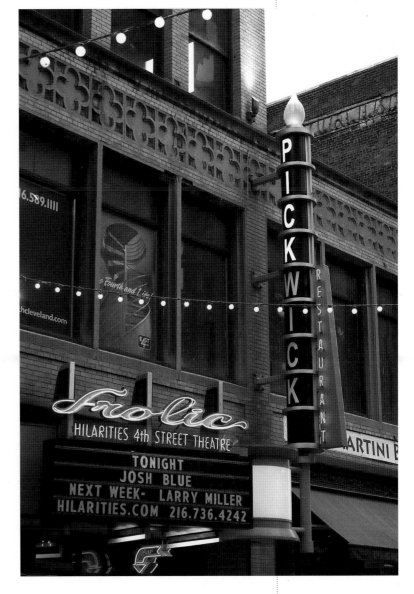

Pickwick & Frolic's distinctive $100,000, 23-foot marquee, illuminated by purple and blue neon lights and extending five feet onto Fourth Street, beckons visitors into the 27,000 square-foot entertainment venue. *(Jay Kossman)*

Kostis acquired training in psychology, later becoming a school psychologist. He progressed to director of pupil personnel in the Tallmadge City School district and then worked for seven years as director of child study in the Oberlin City Schools. During his Oberlin tenure, Kostis founded a vending machine business to supply 100 percent pure fruit juices to schools, health clubs, YMCAs, and similar organizations. The company evolved into a full-line food and beverage supplier. Its success forced Kostis to choose between his professional career in education and the expanding vending machine operation. Kostis selected the business world, adding a line of video games during the Space Invaders and Pac Man era. He sold the company before the collapse of the store-occupied video game business.

Acquiring the name and liquor license from the estate of the owner of the Little Bar on East 9th Street next to the Roxy Theater, Kostis opened a new Little Bar in Cleveland's Warehouse District. Kostis had previously used this space to store a truck for his vending machine operations. In less than one year, he sold the bar to launch a comedy club in Cuyahoga Falls. In 1986, Kostis unveiled the Hilarities Comedy Club in the Warehouse District, continuing as one of the early rehabilitation pioneers of the dilapidated downtown area,

During this period, Kostis would walk down Fourth Street, constantly reminded of the bustling yet intimate streets of his Brooklyn youth. He wondered why Fourth Street never became the successor to Short Vincent, Cleveland's downtown hotspot in the 1940s and 1950s. In

Pickwick & Frolic's Hilarities Fourth Street Theatre, with walls soaring 30 feet, is the largest made-for-comedy showroom in the country. In 2005, *USA Today* selected Hilarities as "one of the ten great places to sit down and watch stand-up." A 20x15-foot sandstone section of the original Euclid Avenue Opera House foundation is to the right in this picture. Kostis purchased the chandelier at the top of the picture from the O'Neil's department store in Akron.
(Jay Kossman)

physical appearance, Fourth Street and Short Vincent shared an uncanny similarity in length, width, and closeness of storefronts. A generation after Short Vincent's popularity, Kostis became an important pioneer in transforming Fourth Street into downtown Cleveland's hippest entertainment district.

In development for more than four years and under construction for 20 months, Nick Kostis' $4.5 million Pickwick & Frolic entertainment center replaced five storefronts, engulfing two floors of the southern portion of the former Kresge complex. Capable of accommodating 900 guests, Pickwick & Frolic is comprised of a 185-seat restaurant, 35-seat bar, 120-seat cabaret, martini bar, champagne bar, and 425-seat comedy club.

Pickwick & Frolic debuted on September 6, 2002, exactly 127 years after the Euclid Avenue Opera House had premiered on the same site. Kostis possesses a keen sense of history; virtually everything in his venue pays tribute to the past. The Pickwick & Frolic name evolved from the Pickwick Restaurant and Frolic Show Bar once located on colorful Short Vincent Street. Another inspiration for the name came from Charles Dickens' *Papers of the Pickwick Club* (commonly called the *Pickwick Papers*) containing humor not characteristic of Dickens' novels. The restaurant's color scheme reflects shades used in old Opera House playbills. Paying more than homage to Cleveland history, Pickwick & Frolic became Fourth Street's first entertainment anchor; its success paved the way for the street's continued renaissance. In 2010, the Ohio Restaurant Association awarded Kostis its prestigious Lifetime Achievement Award for his efforts

On March 7, 2010, Pickwick and Frolic hosted "The Road to the Red Carpet," a fundraiser for the Greater Cleveland Film Commission. Partygoers drank champagne and ate hors d'oeuvres while watching the Academy Award festivities on large-screen televisions. *(Jay Kossman)*

James Todd and Ruth Lohse designed and painted the Food Mural in Pickwick & Frolic's buffet area.
(Michelle Todd)

in revitalizing the Warehouse District and Fourth Street.

During the construction of Pickwick & Frolic, filmmakers used the building as one of the sets for *Welcome to Collinwood*, a motion picture starring George Clooney and written by Cleveland-area natives Joe and Anthony Russo. Kostis met James Todd, a scenic designer working on the film's sets. Impressed with Todd's use of faux techniques, Kostis hired him to help design Pickwick & Frolic's interior. Faux finishes use one material to resemble another; a surface, for example, can be created to look like marble, wood graining, or Venetian plaster by applying paint using streaking techniques. Drawing on Todd's creativity and experience, what appears to be marble in Pickwick & Frolic's interior is probably wood, and what seems to be wood might be drywall.

Todd and fellow artist Ruth Lohse employed unique faux finishes throughout

Pickwick & Frolic's lobby, restaurant, martini bar, buffet area, and the women's restrooms. The main-floor lobby and restaurant design resembles an old hotel or theater from the turn of the 20th Century; the downstairs area captures the look of the 1940s. Requiring more than 3,000 hours of effort, everything from the wooden doors to the walls is hand painted. Pickwick & Frolic's handrails, designed and constructed from scratch, required eight months to create.

Todd painted the pillars at the main bar and the enormous "silver-gilted" mirror in the restaurant. He and Lohse designed and painted two large murals. The Cleveland Mural, near the martini bar, is a collage of Cleveland landmarks dating from the late 19th Century. The "Food Mural," enhancing the buffet area of the comedy club, is a montage of various foods and dishes. A smaller mural features desserts, fruits, and beverages. A 92-foot, hand-tinted "film reel" scrolls above the restaurant's bar. Created and hand-tinted by Todd and artists Bill and Kathy Van, the computer-generated images resemble colorized versions of old movies. Todd also designed the Pickwick & Frolic logo and hand painted many signs throughout this entertainment venue.

Enhancing the interior's nostalgic theme, Kostis purchased four chandeliers, sight unseen, from Akron's closed O'Neil's department store. The restored chandeliers, worth much more than the $1,500 price for each, now sit above the main lobby, ornamental staircase, and Hilarities' stage.

JAMES E. TODD

James E. Todd, born in Cleveland's Tremont neighborhood, began his artistic career by hand painting wooden storefront signs for the Pepsi-Cola Company. After moving to San Francisco, Todd witnessed a performance of *The Music Man* starring Dick Van Dyke. Todd's fascination with the theatrical sets inspired him to pursue set painting and designing as a career. He painted sets for four Disney movies (*Joy Luck Club, Sister Act 2, James and the Giant Peach,* and *Down Periscope*); other motion picture credits ranged from *Mrs. Doubtfire* to *I Married an Axe Murderer*. Most often, Todd repainted brand new sets to achieve a perception of wear and tear, or to create a look reflecting a different time period. Todd also contributed to television commercials (including the LeBron James "King James"

Nike advertisement), tour sets for Stevie Wonder, Jimmy Buffet, Allen Jackson, and others, and cultural organizations including the San Francisco Opera and San Jose Civic Light Opera.

Returning to Cleveland to be closer to his extended family, Todd designed and painted exhibition space for the Western Reserve Historical Society, the Cleveland Museum of Natural History, and the Cleveland Zoo's Australian Outback Adventure. Theater credits include the Cleveland-San Jose Ballet, Cleveland Playhouse, Cleveland Opera, and Great Lakes Theater Festival. He also served as a scenic painter in a series of motion pictures filmed in Cleveland: *Against the Ropes, Antwone Fisher, Welcome to Collinwood,* and *The Oh in Ohio*.

The high-end Kevin Clinton's Martini Bar is under-lit using a process called dichrolam, invented by Clevelander John Blazy. The laminated polymer creates an almost mesmerizing three-dimensional appearance, changing color depending on light source and direction. The innovative Pickwick & Frolic bar is one of the world's first applications of dichrolam.

JOHN BLAZY

As a six-year-old growing up in Chesterland, John Blazy made elaborate geometric designs in mud pies. He later won numerous awards in high school art competitions before earning a degree from the Rochester Institute of Technology, majoring in furniture design. After graduation, Blazy founded a high-end cabinetry business, soon adding hall mirrors to his product offerings. In his innovative mirror designs, Blazy incorporated dichroic glass, a material that amazingly changes colors as the viewing angle is altered. From mirrors, Blazy's use of the fascinating glass expanded; one application involved inlaying dichroic glass into 20 planters he designed for Sherwin Williams' world headquarters lobby.

Blazy, working with a Cleveland company specializing in ultraviolet coatings, developed

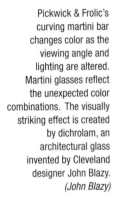

Pickwick & Frolic's curving martini bar changes color as the viewing angle and lighting are altered. Martini glasses reflect the unexpected color combinations. The visually striking effect is created by dichrolam, an architectural glass invented by Cleveland designer John Blazy.
(John Blazy)

a dramatically cost-effective alternative process to manufacture dichroic glass. The traditional method entailed using a laser to vaporize metallic oxides in a vacuum chamber, allowing the molecules to coat the surface of the glass. Blazy substituted films that could be textured, glued together, and placed on glass or plastic. The processed film created dramatic color changing properties without the costly use of vacuum chambers or lasers. In addition to lowering costs, the process eliminated size constraints previously inherent with dichroic glass and also reduced surface vulnerability. Blazy called his new product dichrolam.

Since the Pickwick & Frolic application, the material has been used in the construction of walls, skylights, and conference tables for an impressive list of clients including Disney, Sony Style, MTV, the Tampa Hard Rock Café, the Oklahoma City Federal Building, Bloomberg Financial Executive Offices, WPP / Y&R (the world's largest advertising group), Norwegian Star Cruise Lines, and numerous libraries and children's hospitals in Ohio, New York, Massachusetts, North Carolina, and Hawaii.

The House of Blues

House of Blues, operating 12 live music concert halls and restaurants throughout the U.S., opened its 42,000-square-foot Cleveland facility on November 19, 2004. The complex includes a 1,200-person capacity music hall, a 300-seat restaurant, and six bars. The music hall hosts a wide variety of acts, including rock, alternative, rap, country, gospel, folk, jazz, and tribute bands. Performers in Cleveland have ranged from Tom Jones, Cheap Trick, and Cyndi Lauper to Three Inches of Blood and Sick Puppies. The restaurant is noted for Creole seafood ambalaya, Cajun meat loaf, North Atlantic Salmon stuffed with shrimp, fried buttermilk battered chicken with country gravy and mashed potatoes, strip steaks, and filet mignon. The Foundation Room, a members-only area, includes a dining room, a media room with a large screen plasma television, and small rooms used for business meetings.

The Corner Alley

Urban bowling alleys, once known for cheap beer and cigarette smoke, now cater to customers seeking designer bowling bags, vintage bowling shoes, and pricey martinis. Fourth Street's upscale bowling establishment is the Corner Alley, a 25,000-square-foot, $6 million bowling facility that opened on December 7, 2006. *Bowlers Journal International*, the bible of the bowling world, selected the Corner Alley among the Top 20 bowling centers you must visit before you die. A private "Millionaires' Row" area contains four lanes and a pool table; a "spare room" is available for company meetings and presentations.

Will Greenwood, an award-winning Southern California chef, created the menu for the accompanying 100-seat restaurant. Greenwood, a White House chef for Bill Clinton, also cooked for both Bush presidents. He prepared meals for Julia Child's 80th birthday celebration, several James Beard Award Celebrations, the American Institute of Food and Wine convention, the America Beef Council Biannual National Press Celebration Dinner, and the Country Music Awards ceremony. Greenwood has been the subject of cover articles in *Gourmet*, *Bon Appetit*, *Chocolatier*, and *People Magazine*. His prestigious awards include Best Chef in America from the American Academy of

The House of Blues restaurant fronts Fourth Street while the adjoining concert hall faces Euclid Avenue. *(Alan Dutka collection)*

Restaurants and Chef of the Year from the National Restaurant Association.

The Corner Alley's appetizers include beer-battered pickle chips, banana peppers stuffed with ground beef, calamari, crab cakes, and Cajun beer-battered crayfish. The menu offers salads, pizzas, pasta, burgers, sandwiches, and entrees featuring steaks, meat loaf, salmon, chicken, and ribs. Among the 29 martini selections are Hep Cat (berry-flavored vodka combined with sweet and dry vermouth), Bubbles & Pears (Absolut pear vodka, champagne, and pear juice) and Banana Cream Pie (Bacardi rum, banana Liqueur, and Godiva white chocolate). Signature drinks include the Corner Alley Striker (berry vodka, Grand Marnier, Chambord, and melon liqueur, Malibu rum, amaretto, and cranberry and pineapple juices), Angel's Temptation (tequila shaken with orange, lime, and apple Juices) and Honolulu

Juicer (Southern Comfort and dark rum mixed with lemon and lime juices).

The Temporary Fourth Street Exhibition Center

After recruiting three vital anchor entertainment venues, the Marons filled the majority of Fourth Street's remaining storefront space with high-profile restaurants. MRN then returned to the anchor entertainment concept, converting the Windsor Block's 14,000 square-feet of storefront space into a temporary exhibition area. *Bodies: The Exhibition*, launched the new site on June 5, 2010, with a seven-month run.

The educational exhibit, comprised of twelve complete bodies and about 250 individual parts, all preserved using a special process, generated interest from the general public and groups of curious nurses, medical assistants, lawyers, and

Located on the corner of Euclid Avenue and Fourth Street, the Corner Alley occupies the space that once housed the largest Kresge variety store in the United States.
(Alan Dutka collection)

A sculpture representing a phoenix, located on the corner of Fourth Street and Euclid Avenue, signifies the rebirth of Fourth Street. A twin sculpture is located on the corner of Fourth Street and Prospect Avenue.
(James A. Toman)

and mice, a pig circus, a legless acrobat, a reptilian contortionist, 90-year-old twin sisters, and a real North Pole village.

Sunday Morning Pioneers

Downtown Cleveland may never regain the amazing vibe of the 1940s when couples waited at 2:00 a.m. for streetcars or buses after a midnight movie at Playhouse Square or an evening of partying on Short Vincent Street. Even in the 1950s, St. John's Cathedral attracted worshipers to its midnight Mass after Catholics enjoyed a fun-filled Saturday night downtown. But Fourth Street today is developing a surprisingly energetic Sunday morning constituency.

At 7:00 a.m., Cleveland's Downtown Ambassadors begin cleaning the sidewalks and watering Fourth Street's decorative plantings, as they do seven days a week. The Erie Island Coffee Shop unlocks its doors at 9:00 a.m.; the earliest arrivals tend to be downtown dwellers and hotel guests. One Fourth Street resident consumes a cup of latte coffee and breakfast sandwich which he describes as a "hangover killer."

In 2007, as urban churches throughout the city faced threats of closure, the Gateway Church launched a downtown house of worship on April Fool's Day in the Pickwick & Frolic Comedy Club. Power Point displays and a contemporary Christian music ensemble replace traditional church bulletins and organists, creating an atmosphere especially appealing to the 20-something target market. The online company eHarmony played a pivotal role in the creation of the new church.

Born in Springfield, Missouri, Alex Ennes grew up near Little Rock, Arkansas. Preparing for a calling to the ministry he nourished since the eighth grade, Ennes graduated from Ouachita Baptist University

school children. Skeletons occupied the spaces where full-length mannequins once enticed clothing shoppers to the Philipsborn store and later the Lerner's and Petrie's dress shops. Specimens of diseased brains, lungs, and livers sat near the location of the first Woolworth lunch counter. After this one solitary display, offices replaced the exhibition center.

Strangely enough, this same space once touted a late-19th-Century exhibition center. In 1893, the Kohl & Middleton's Dime Museum fascinated Clevelanders with attractions including a child with a large head, an armless cowboy who fired his gun using his feet, performing rats (the number-one ranked baccalaureate college in the south according to *U.S. News and World Report*), earning a double major in Christian studies and music; the violin is his musical specialty. Ennes then obtained a master's degree from Southwestern Baptist Theological Seminary in Fort Worth.

Working as a youth minister in Arkansas, Ennes used eHarmony to help match his personality and interests with those of a compatible female. The online technology introduced Ennes to Shari, a Westlake resident and a daughter of a minister. The two eventually met in Cleveland, spending the 2004 Easter weekend at the zoo and her father's North Olmsted church. With an engagement ring and violin in hand, Alex proposed to his future bride on the serene shores of Arkansas's Lake LeGray in July of the same year; they married in the fall. Alex ministered at the North Olmsted Friends Church, but harbored a passion to organize a new church in an urban setting.

A typical Gateway Sunday service consists of a gospel-inspired sermon and Christian music, led by two singers with accompaniment provided by two electric guitarists and a drummer. About half of the church's approximately 100 members are suburbanites. Many joined the church while living downtown. The youthful congregation includes business owners, bankers and accountants with MBA degrees, and doctors, including both an OB/GYN and an anesthetist. Ennis playfully observes the church is an outstanding location for pregnant females, offering expertise in both the delivery of newborns and in administering the proper drugs.

The Gateway Church emphasizes religious worship and community service. Volunteers have planted flowers and cherry trees downtown, packed literally tons of food for distribution to needy people in Northeast Ohio, and sponsored youth activities for inner-city children. The church also supports missionary work in Northeast Ohio and throughout the world. Gateway will soon open a downtown café and coffeehouse. The profits are designated to support additional community service projects.

The House of Blues' gospel brunch, another inspirational Sunday morning activity on Fourth Street, proved less enduring. East Tech graduate Tina Farmer and the Singin' Saints provided rousing music as Sunday morning diners waved their napkins, clapped their hands, and enjoyed a 25-foot buffet filled with pastries, salads, biscuits and gravy, omelets (including a crawfish tail and cheddar concoction), prime rib, and southern fried chicken. Originally supporting two sittings each Sunday morning, the gospel brunch attendance lessened as the novelty waned, necessitating a reduction to one sitting. Today, the gospel brunch is only offered on holidays and special occasions such as Mothers' Day.

Pickwick and Frolic and the House of Blues are two of Fourth Street's entertainment anchors. *(James A. Toman)*

Chapter VI
Celebrity Chefs

TIMELINE

2006	Lola
2007	Wonder Bar, Zocalo Mexican Grill & Tequileria
2008	Saigon Restaurant & Bar, La Strada
2009	Erie Island Coffee Shop, Greenhouse Tavern
2010	Chinato
2011	Dredgers Union, Cleveland Visitors Center

Cleveland produced its share of superstars in the 20th Century, including such sports heroes as Bob Feller, Jim Brown, Otto Graham, and Jesse Owens. Marcus Hanna and Newton B. Baker profoundly influenced the national political scene while Bob Hope entertained world-wide audiences for almost a century.

In addition to the traditional avenues for hero worship, Clevelanders celebrated a few quirky and unique offshoots. The Cleveland Ballet marketed a set of trading cards, patterned after the familiar format for baseball luminaries, to honor each member of their talented dance troupe. On another occasion, a jubilant late-night crowd flocked to Cleveland's airport to greet their conquering champions returning from a triumphant road trip; the Cleveland Orchestra had just completed a European tour that generated rave reviews. Although Cleveland may rank high in producing sports stars, entertainers, and first-class cultural organizations, famous chefs have, until very recently, been much rarer on the local scene.

In the 20th Century, Hector Boiardi (who would become known as Chef Boy-ar-dee) may have been Cleveland's best known professional cook. Chef Hector, serving as head of New York's Plaza Hotel restaurant, earned praise from the chancellor of Italy who called Boiardi the world's greatest chef. In 1915, Boiardi supervised the catering of President Woodrow Wilson's wedding. Coming to Cleveland, he

Award-winning chef Michael Symon opened the Lola restaurant on Fourth Street in 2006. *(James A. Toman)*

Saigon Restaurant & Bar offers authentic Vietnamese cuisine and exotic Asian cocktails. *(Ken Ho)*

continued to perfect his skills at the Hotel Winton on Prospect Avenue before opening Il Giardino d'Italia, at East Ninth Street and Woodland Avenue in the 1920s. He moved his restaurant to the basement of a building located at the intersection of three forbidding alleys between Euclid and Prospect avenues just west of East Ninth Street. Disproving the restaurant adage that location is everything, hungry Clevelanders navigated their way through desolate passageways to devour Chef Hector's food from 1931 to 1967. After the restaurant finally shuttered its doors, four decades elapsed before Michael Symon emerged as Cleveland's next full-fledged celebrity chef.

Raised in North Olmsted, Symon graduated from Lakewood's Saint Edward High School, where a broken arm shattered his aspirations to earn a college wrestling scholarship in order to study landscape architecture or teaching. After obtaining a part-time cooking position at Gepetto's Ribs on Warren Road, Symon needed

only ten years to build a national culinary reputation. After his graduation from the Culinary Institute of America, he learned his trade at several Northeast Ohio restaurants including Player's, Piccolo Mondo, Giovanni's, and the Caxton Cafe. In 1997, he opened Lola, his own restaurant, in the Tremont neighborhood. Within one year, *Restaurant Hospitality Magazine* called him a national rising star and *Food & Wine* magazine named Symon one of the ten best new chefs in America. The *New York Times* used the words "energetic," "inventive," and "terrific" to describe Lola.

The lure of Fourth Street enticed Symon to relocate his Tremont triumph. In 2005, he converted Tremont's Lola into Lolita and reopened Lola on Fourth Street the following year. Solid economic rationale justified the move downtown. His Tremont venue, often booked solid six weeks in advance, accommodated 65 diners; the larger downtown location seated 105. Although the price of dinners declined at the more casual Lolita, dining turnover increased because the more informal atmosphere reduced the time to consume meals.

Symon's super-chef stature increased dramatically in the next few years as he escalated to prominence on television's Food Network. The network chose Symon to participate in its popular reality program *Next Iron Chef.* Appearing as a contestant is an honor in itself because the Food Network and current Iron Chefs hand-select each contestant. Symon won the 2007 contest by defeating his opponents in criteria consisting of speed, artistry, simplicity, innovation,

resourcefulness, creativity under pressure, leadership, and attaining greatness. His tasks included deboning a chicken, opening a coconut, preparing six one-bite dishes, making desserts from catfish tripe, crafting dishes incorporating xanthan gum, and creating a meal for a party in France honoring the U.S. Ambassador. Symon's final challenge involved developing a dinner made from swordfish.

He gained a permanent position on *Iron Chef America*, a one-hour cooking competition; he hosted *Dinner: Impossible*, demonstrated his culinary expertise on more than 100 episodes of *Melting Pot*, and appeared on *Food Nation; Sara's*

The Greenhouse Tavern's five drop lights are custom-made from recycled bicycle rims. *(Amelia Zatik Sawyer)*

At the rear of Zocalo's main floor is the bar. The ornate railing borders a curving staircase which leads to additional patron seating on the lower level.
(James A. Toman)

Secrets; and *Ready, Set, Cook*. Not limiting himself to the Food Network, Symon's credits also include a Cleveland episode of Travel Channel's *Anthony Bourdain: No Reservations* and articles in *Bon Appetit, Esquire, Food Arts, Gourmet, Saveur,* and *O, The Oprah Magazine.* He even promoted a Nintendo video game called *Cook or Be Cooked*.

In 2009, Symon achieved another triumph by capturing a James Beard Foundation Gold Medal for the Best Chef in the Great Lakes region. Deemed "the Oscars of the food world" by *Time* magazine, James Beard awards are the country's most coveted honor for chefs, restaurants, food and beverage professionals, as well as for media,

architects, and designers working in the food industry. During the award's 19-year history, Symon became the first winner among Cleveland chefs. The following year, Symon hosted his own program, *Cook Like an Iron Chef*, on television's new Cooking Channel. He is also a spokesperson for Vita-Mix blenders and Calphalon cookware.

Featuring American cuisine, diners at Lola choose among lobster, oysters, and crispy bone marrow for appetizers. Entrée specialties feature scallops, sturgeon, arctic char, walleye, duck, smoked Berkshire pork chop, port shank, beef hanger steak, rib eye, and roasted chicken. The "6 A. M. Special," a popular dessert, features French toast with maple-bacon ice cream.

Lola's 2006 opening paved the way for eight carefully selected additions to Fourth Street's growing persona: Wonder Bar (August 6, 2007), Zocalo Mexican Grill & Tequileria (September 6, 2007), Saigon Restaurant & Bar (February 22, 2008), La Strada (November 22, 2008), Erie Island Coffee Shop (February 19, 2009), Greenhouse Tavern (April 13, 2009), and Chinato (January 20, 2010).

The **Wonder Bar** is Fourth Street's version of an upscale neighborhood hangout. The extensive drink selection features Death in the Afternoon, a cocktail created by Ernest Hemingway, who authored a novel by the same name; Between the Sheets, a mixture of rum, cognac and citronge liqueur; and an assortment of vodka-flavored martinis. Beer offerings feature Great Lakes Brewing Company favorites and an array of specialty brews including Rogue's Morimoto Soba

and Dead Guy ale from Oregon, Dogfish Festina Peche from Delaware, Left Hand Polestar Pilsner from Colorado, Young's Double Chocolate Stout from Britain, and Lindemann's Framboise from Belgium. Wines include Chardonnay and rose wines from France, Tawny Porto from Portugal, and Muscat dessert wine from California.

The Wonder Bar selected rising luminary Michael Walsh as its initial chef. Walsh attended Ohio Wesleyan University, pursuing an education in microbiology, but he eventually concluded kitchens created more excitement than laboratories. His resume featured experience at some of Cleveland's finer restaurants including the Blue Point, Baricelli Inn, and Fahrenheit. He has served dinners to John Glenn and Michael Jordan. Lacking complete kitchen facilities at the Wonder Bar, Walsh creatively utilized a convection oven, sandwich press, and tabletop burners

Two beautiful glass panes (right) capture the look and feel of Italy as customers enter the Chinato restaurant. *(Kevin Reeves/Westlake Reed Leskosky)*

Left: Colorful signage adds excitement to Fourth Street's ambiance. *(James A. Toman)*

Right: Looking north toward Euclid Avenue, a summer lunch crowd is beginning to assemble at the popular Zocalo Mexican Grill and Tequileria. *(Alan Dutka collection)*

to create appetizing offerings, including oxtail stew, served in terracotta crocks and earthenware. After about one year, Walsh resigned to accept a chef's position in Avon.

The bar, rarely open for lunch, does not achieve the same culinary status as its neighbors. But its diverse evening entertainment, including reggae, blues, and jazz, attracts lively crowds. Recalling a bygone Fourth Street era, the Wonder Bar also offers palm readings, handwriting analysis, tarot card readings, E.S.P. readings, energy crystal readings, aura energy readings, crystal ball readings, and full-life readings.

The **Zocalo Mexican Grill & Tequileria** offers a menu created by Aaron Sanchez, a James Beard Foundation nominee for Rising Star Chef of the Year award and *People En Español's* selection as one of its 50 Most Beautiful People. Sanchez, a finalist in the 2007 *Next Iron Chef* competition, placed fourth behind winner Michael Symon. A former co-host of Food Network's *Melting Pot*, Sanchez owns two acclaimed restaurants in New York City (Paladar and Centrico). He authored *La Comida del Barrio*, a cookbook exploring

unique local cuisines and culture specific to Latin-American neighborhoods across the United States, including Miami's Little Havana, New York's Spanish Harlem, and San Francisco's Mission.

Zocalo's food menu, accompanied by 99 different tequilas and 26 unique margaritas, highlights unique recipes native to three culinary regions of Mexico: Yucatan, Puebla, and Veracruz. Yucatan is noted for using recipes combining black beans and pumpkin seeds with fresh meats and vegetables; the menu features carnitas (pork shoulder smothered in achiote rub) and Tikin-Xic (stewed seafood with spicy chipotle sauce). Puebla is represented by chiles rellenos (poblano peppers stuffed with cheese) and meat-stuffed tamales. Veracruz is noted for seafood native to coastal waters. The menu highlights huachinango a la veracruzana (regional fish with spicy tomato sauce), escabeche (fresh scallops, calamari, and baby rock shrimp steamed in Dos Equis beer and chilled in a habanero-lime-orange-cilantro marinade), and fresh flour tortillas stuffed with marinated grilled shrimp with spicy tomatillo mayonnaise.

The **Saigon Restaurant & Bar** story begins with the emigration of three Vietnamese families to Philadelphia. Bon Thei, a member of the South Vietnamese army, remained in a Vietnam penitentiary for 18 months after the fall of Saigon, imprisoned by barbed wire and by the threat of hungry tigers prowling outside the stockade. After Thei's release, his family, including his four sisters, immigrated to Philadelphia. Kenny Ho, reaching Philadelphia at the age of 12, worked in one of the city's first authentic Vietnamese restaurants while in high school. Danny Nguyen, moving to Philadelphia during his high school years, later owned a Vietnamese restaurant.

The three immigrants' friendship began when Kenny and Danny found themselves dating two of Bon Thei's sisters, whom they each eventually married. Bon, after a successful eight-year career with Philadelphia Energy, voluntarily accepted an employment buyout. He then moved to Cleveland and founded Creative Nails, one of the area's most successful nail care businesses. From the original location in the Lee-Harvard neighborhood, Bon expanded his business with additional locations on Lorain Road and in Mentor. Kenny and Danny moved to Cleveland to participate in their brother-in-law's growing prosperity.

The trio, envisioning a greater opportunity as restaurant proprietors, opened the acclaimed #1 Pho on Superior Avenue in Cleveland's Asiatown district. Saigon, their second restaurant, offers authentic Vietnamese dishes influenced by China, Thailand, and France. Appetizers and entrées feature creative combinations of pork, beef, chicken, tofu, shrimp, squid, red snapper, catfish, vegetables, rice, and soup.

La Strada is owned by Terry Tarantino, whose roots lie squarely in

Sixteen bowling lanes are the most prominent feature of the Corner Alley. The facility also houses a billiards room, two bars, and a restaurant.
(James A. Toman)

La Strada's décor is based on a Mediterranean motif. Two levels of seating occupy the first floor, and a balcony level provides additional seating.
(James A. Toman)

Italy; his mother's side of the family resides near Rome and his father's branch near Naples. A third-generation native of Cleveland's Little Italy, Tarantino developed an early respect for gardening, an admiration partially fostered by a grandfather proficient in farming and a godfather engaged in landscaping. Very bright, exceptionally personable, and aggressive, at an early age he displayed an ability to merge business instincts with family heritage. As a 12-year-old *Plain Dealer* carrier, Tarantino designed, planted, and maintained a vegetable garden for one of his newspaper customers. Under his skilled guidance and management, Tarantino's client received the morning news, along with a garden brimming with fresh tomatoes, cucumbers, and peppers.

Expanding on his youthful passion, Tarantino established his own landscaping business immediately after earning a degree in horticulture from Ohio State University. After spending a decade designing landscapes, Tarantino's creative ideas greatly surpassed his customers' decidedly more mundane requirements, a situation leading to a career change that resulted in his acclaimed *La Dolce Vita* restaurant in Little Italy.

Traveling to Turkey to help a friend launch a new restaurant, Tarantino gained an appreciation for Mediterranean cuisine, culture, and scenery. He returned to Cleveland motivated to establish a bistro reflecting the image of a Turkish street at dusk. La Strada is the result of Tarantino's original inspiration.

Customers entering La Strada immediately encounter a long aisle bisecting the eating space and extending the length of the restaurant, appropriately suggesting "the street," (which is the English translation for the restaurant's name). Tarantino considered painting a double-yellow line down this symbolic corridor – the same passageway once containing a myriad of enticing bargains for Woolworth shoppers – but opted for more subtle tactics. To the left, dining tables rest in an elevated area, accompanied by additional eating space at floor level as the aisle continues. The setting is intended to beckon hungry diners to enjoy the taste of Mediterranean food and the feel of an exotic landscape. To the right, a winding staircase with a wrought-iron banister leads to a second level flanked with accompanying wrought-iron railings, where diners gaze down upon a projection of Fellini's 1954 classic movie *La Strada* or the 1942 Academy Award winning *Casablanca*, almost imitating the experience of sitting in the balcony of a bygone movie theater. A bar, situated below the second level, is artfully integrated in the overall street scene illusion.

In contrast to typical sports or music memorabilia, Mediterranean-inspired artwork and art objects fill the restaurant's stucco and Venetian-plaster walls. Subtle lighting emanates from candles, backlit walls, and stained-glass windows, while one large chandelier, near the end of the simulated street, supplies direct light. It blends with a creatively painted wall to suggest a setting sun casting its deep orange glow, the onset of a somehow mysterious Turkish evening.

The menu, about 30 percent Italian, also incorporates Mediterranean influences from Spain, Morocco, Turkey, Portugal, Greece, and Albania. Each item's name suggests, directly or indirectly, a geographic inspiration: antipasto dishes are named Insalata di Roma, Greek peasant, and Turkish domates. Pastas include Fettuccini Fellini, marinara, and tortellini. Kabobs are offered in beef, chicken, and lamb. Entrees feature Grecian roughy,

Samak-Casablanca (fish), Bistesca del Giomac (steak), and Barcelona skirt (a combination of veal sausage, mussels, and skirt steak).

The history of the **Erie Island Coffee Shop** begins on Kelleys Island, located four miles off Lake Erie's shore and 12 miles northwest of Sandusky. The beautiful sanctuary is perfect for swimming, hiking, fishing, and bicycling. Compared to Cleveland, life is definitely more relaxed in this community of about 350 year-around residents. A major tourist attraction is watching monarch butterflies and migratory birds. Total enrollment in the school system, offering kindergarten through twelfth grade, is approximately 30 students. The Chamber of Commerce allows its computer to be used for E-mail correspondence, but only during daytime office hours. This unpretentious environment offered an ideal refuge for semi-retired Alan Glazen.

In 1972, Glazen's Creative Studios started as an advertising agency, eventually evolving into a hybrid ad agency and video production company. Anticipating a gradual retirement, Glazen purchased a log home on Kelleys Island, steadily spending more time at his summer retreat. When the local coffee shop proprietor abandoned the business, the building's owner became increasingly more frustrated managing the store, eventually offering it to Glazen. With no experience in either the coffee business or retail store ownership, Glazen relied on three partners to fill the gaps in his expertise.

Photographer Martin Reuben, a professional acquaintance of Glazen's for decades, originally came to Cleveland from Florida to assist a well-known photographer catering to business clients. Eventually Ruben founded TRG Studios to provide photographic services

A cup of freshly-brewed latte coffee is prepared by a friendly employee of the Erie Island Coffee Shop. *(Alan Dutka collection)*

Annalie Glazen, Alan's daughter-in-law, contributed her extensive retail coffee background to the ownership team. As a 15-year-old high school student, Annalie rode her bicycle down Lake Road at four in the morning to her part-time job at Cravings, a coffeehouse located in an old Rocky River greenhouse. Later employed by Starbucks while earning her college degree, she eventually managed six Cleveland shops.

Scott Stevenson, Glazen's third partner, is a retired ferryboat captain and year-around resident of Kelleys Island. Although Stevenson made important contributions during the busy summer tourist season, his local "insider" intelligence proved even more valuable. Getting tasks accomplished on an island requires an understanding of local logistics, along with knowledge of who might provide needed assistance. When an emergency repair is needed, there is no Kelleys Island hardware store to purchase a hammer or nails. The island is accessed by a commercial ferryboat, private boats, or airplanes. One of these is required to travel to Sandusky for the nearest hardware store. Since no transportation is formally scheduled to and from the airport, commuters often rent golf carts to travel between the airfield and business area.

The 300-square-foot Erie Island Coffee Shop opened at the beginning of the 2008 tourist season. In the first three months, appreciative customers purchased 25,000 cups of coffee. The Fourth Street shop opened in 2009. Six times larger than the Kelleys Island location, it offers brewed coffee, espresso drinks, real-fruit smoothies, soups, salads, and sandwiches. Downtown workers, neighborhood residents, tourists, and Gateway entertainment visitors enjoy specialties, including chocolate raspberry

to businesses. Glazen recruited Ruben for his impending coffee venture, not for his photographic skills but because of his passionate quest to discover the perfectly-brewed coffee. Using a coffee roaster vented through the ceiling of his business, Ruben mixes different varieties of coffee beans, brewing the concoctions for various lengths of time and at differing temperatures. Glazen refers to his partner as the mad scientist of coffee making, but Ruben downplays his expertise, describing his coffee roaster as nothing more than an oversexed popcorn popper.

mocha and white chocolate coconut frappe. The coffee shop personnel intentionally create a friendly, neighborhood atmosphere very difficult to duplicate in larger coffee houses owned by corporate chains.

Just five months after the French-inspired **Greenhouse Tavern** opened in 2009, *Bon Appetit* magazine selected it as one of the ten best new restaurants in America. The potato-crusted goat cheese tarts with heirloom tomato salad received special praise. In the same month, *Restaurant Hospitality* lauded owner Jonathon Sawyer by commenting, "This guy's not just embracing the hottest trends in the restaurant business, he's helping to define them." Before the Greenhouse Tavern celebrated its first anniversary, *Food & Wine Magazine* selected Sawyer as one of the ten best new chefs in America, the same honor bestowed upon Michael Symon a dozen years earlier.

Jonathon Sawyer, born in Chicago, moved to Strongsville at the age of seven. On his 13th birthday, he obtained his first job, frying tortilla chips and rolling cornflakes around ice cream in a Strongsville restaurant. Sawyer has been in the restaurant business ever since. After graduating from Strongsville High School, Sawyer enrolled in the industrial engineering program at the University of Dayton, but, after two years, decided to pursue his true passion. After graduating from the Pennsylvania Culinary Institute in Pittsburgh, Sawyer joined the restaurant at the Biltmore Hotel in Miami. One year later, he worked alongside celebrated master chef Charlie Palmer in four New York restaurants (Kitchen 22, Aureole, Astra, and Kitchen 82). Following his work in New York with Charlie Palmer, Sawyer became the first chef at Michael Symon's Lolita restaurant in Tremont. Returning to New York, he opened Symon's Parea

restaurant. In 2007, Sawyer established his own restaurant, Bar Cento, in Ohio City.

The Greenhouse Tavern's appetizers feature French breakfast radishes, red-wine-braised olives, steamed clams, hand-ground beef tartare frites, braised lamb shank ravioli, and "Devils on Horseback," composed of bacon-wrapped dates, almonds, bitter chocolate, and roasted

Outdoor diners (left and below) enjoy lunch at the nationally acclaimed Greenhouse Tavern. *(Alan Dutka collection)*

fresno pepper. Entrées include an Ohio beef burger, steak or lamb frites, pork chops, chicken, pasta, fish, and both a vegan and vegetarian dish. The dessert menu contains triple chocolate cake, pear and cranberry crisp, and apple pine nut tarte tatin.

Sawyer's dedication to environmental consciousness culminated in Ohio's first LEED-certified (Leadership in Energy and Environmental Design) restaurant. The renovation of the Cort Building and subsequent creation of the Greenhouse Tavern incorporated environmentally friendly decisions at every stage. The restaurant contains four distinct dining areas: a first-floor section, two mezzanines, and a basement. Virtually everything used in creating the décor has been recycled: seventeen old doors are now dividers, bar facing, service stations, and table tops. Salvaged hardwood rotors serve as partitions. The concrete floor uses reclaimed ash, originally a waste product of an electrical power station's smoke stacks. The bar top is made of concrete composed of recycled glass, mainly windows and wine and beer bottles, broken into bits and manufactured on site. Storage units above the bar are reclaimed from educational and government buildings. Oak flooring has been recycled into bar stools, chairs, and shelves. Custom-built light fixtures use old bicycle rims. The stairs leading to the mezzanines are made of recycled tire rubber. Carpet squares in the mezzanines use samples ordered by interior designers and architects that otherwise would have been discarded. In the basement, oak tables attained new lives after serving in science classrooms at John Carroll University in the 1950s. The menu is printed on 100 percent recycled fiber. Continuing the environmental theme, water-saving technologies are used in the bars, kitchen, and rest rooms. The faucets utilize motion sensors and the rest rooms employ solar-powered flushers and faucets.

Charlie Palmer, an early advocate of acquiring food from local farms, influenced Sawyer's decision to make use of neighboring food providers. Sawyer believes the quality of the restaurant's food is related to the proximity of the food source. The Greenhouse's meats, fruits, and vegetables originate from Ohio farms. Potato vodka is a product of Pennsylvania while Buffalo Trace bourbon comes from Kentucky.

Carrying the recycling and locally grown themes to an even higher level, Sawyer designed a rooftop urban garden above the Greenhouse Tavern. The restaurant's food wastes are composted into dirt where herbs and vegetables are grown for use in the restaurant's salads. The garden is watered from rain water captured by barrels located on the restaurant's roof.

Although Jonathon Sawyer is too young to remember Fourth Street's retail stores, his grandmother recalls purchasing shoes at Cort's shoe store, the storefront now containing the first-floor dining room and bar of her grandson's award-winning restaurant.

Chinato is the creation of Zack Bruell, a Shaker Heights High School graduate and one of Cleveland's most noted chefs. Bruell attended the University of Pennsylvania's Wharton School of Finance to prepare for an expected future career in his father's hardware business. Unimpressed with the school cafeteria, Bruell cooked his own meals using a hot plate and toaster oven. Drafted at the age of 19 during the Vietnam conflict, he followed his military service by completing a degree in business at the University of Colorado. His interest in cooking escalated when he met a fellow student who had attended Le Cordon Bleu, the coveted culinary academy in Paris.

After finishing college, Bruell enrolled in Philadelphia's Restaurant School and later launched the 20th Street Café, a Philadelphia restaurant generating nationwide attention. Next, Bruell joined Michael's, an acclaimed restaurant in Santa Monica. In the late 1970s and early 1980s, Bruell and other chefs at Michael's pioneered bistro dining and fusion cuisine.

Bruell then returned to Cleveland, accepting a position with Executive Caterers at Landerhaven. Three years later, he founded Z Contemporary Cuisine in Shaker Heights. That restaurant received praise in *The New York Times, USA Today, Food & Wine, Art Culinaire,* and *Nation's Restaurant News.* After a decade of working 80-hour weeks, Bruell sold the restaurant to devote more time to his family and golf game. After working as top chef at Ken Stewart's in Akron, a rejuvenated Bruell established three Cleveland restaurants, each receiving national acclaim. Parallax, in the Tremont neighborhood, earned *Wine Spectator* magazine's praise as "the big hit of the year"; *Esquire* magazine selected Table 45 at the InterContinental Hotel as a Best New Restaurant; and *USA Today* praised L'Albatros Brasserie, a French restaurant in University Circle. During his career, Bruell has been nominated for three James Beard awards.

Chinato, established in 2010, takes its name from an Italian after-dinner wine flavored with bark from the cinchona tree. The décor of the 150-seat restaurant is reminiscent of Italy in the 1920s. One wall contains a 10-by-35-foot mural of Florence. Bruell's goal of crafting an illusion of an old sepia photograph became a reality with creative contributions from the Epstein Design Partners. Two glass columns, containing scenes of Venice, welcome customers as they enter the restaurant. One wall in the main restaurant area is dominated by a 10-by-35-foot mural of the Florence cityscape as viewed from a nearby hill. Another mural in a downstairs banquet room presents a collage of images from Italy. Creating a unified theme, the images throughout the restaurant also embellish the menus and wine lists.

Chinato offers food typical of that found in Italy's upscale restaurants. Dinner begins with crudo, an appetizer containing raw fish (scallops, yellowtail, tuna, or salmon). Antipasti feature soups, vegetables, or fish. Pasta dishes include linguine with baby clams, spaghetti with mixed shellfish, and ravioli with pork or veal. Entrees incorporate chicken, beef, lamb, or fish. Examples are Venetian-style calves liver with dried figs, lamb stew in tomato broth, beef braised in Amarone, stuffed Swordfish with olive paste, brick-flattened chicken breast with panzanella salad, and whole-roasted chicken with truffle honey glaze, The menu also features creative salads and pizza. Dessert favorites include tiramisu, ricotta cheesecake, lemon polenta cake, almond panna cotta, and chocolate hazelnut mousse cake.

Zack Bruell never joined his father's hardware business. Initially, Ernest Bruell strongly disagreed with his son's career choice but lived to witness Zack's success as a chef and restaurant owner. Ernest died of lung cancer in1984; eight years later the Cleveland Clinic initiated the Ernest Bruell Memorial Lecture, an annual address by a prominent researcher in the field of lung cancer research. Zack conducted fund-raising events at his restaurants to help launch the memorial. On the evening before each lecture, Zack hosts a dinner for the speaker and Cleveland Clinic staff members at one of his restaurants.

Epilogue

Following the publication of this book, East Fourth Street's evolution continued with two significant new developments: a cutting-edge retail establishment now occupies the old McCrory variety store space while Positively Cleveland's Visitor Information Center and offices reside in the former temporary exhibition area. With these additions, Fourth Street is now home to retail and offices, as well as its award-winning entertainment and restaurant venues.

Although retail has not kept pace with downtown Cleveland's rebirth as an entertainment center, Danielle DeBoe and Sean Bilovecky, two 30-something entrepreneurs, have taken a significant step to enhance downtown retailing options. The Dredgers Union, a combined apparel and home goods lifestyle center, opened in the summer 2011. Characteristic of its Fourth Street neighbors, the Dredgers Union shopping experience is not easily duplicated in suburban malls. The store offers a private label for men's and women's apparel, designed in Cleveland and manufactured in the U.S. Whenever possible, the owners purchase locally produced merchandise, ranging from apparel to bedding and kitchen gadgets. American-made bicycles are complemented with apparel especially designed for cyclists. Most importantly, DeBoe and Bilovecky understand urban retailing and Fourth Street's unique high-energy environment; DeBoe has even made her home in a Fourth Street apartment.

DeBoe, a native of Euclid, Ohio, worked in Los Angeles after attending Kent State University. Concentrating on the production of television commercials and music videos, she gained experience in the prop, wardrobe, and set departments. Returning to Cleveland, DeBoe enhanced her experience first as a buyer for Cottonwood, a Chagrin Falls interior design and furniture establishment, and then as visual manager for Anthropologie in the Eaton Collection on Chagrin Boulevard. Next, DeBoe opened Room Service, her own boutique.

Bilovecky, born in Munroe Falls, Ohio, also attended Kent State. Capitalizing on his expertise in fashion design, he and a partner founded Wrath Arcane, a menswear label offering merchandise

designed and manufactured in the U.S. The label acquired a passionate following in the United Kingdom, Ireland, Italy, Australia, Japan, and Singapore, as well as the U.S. But many small boutiques, the core of the company's sales, collapsed during the severe worldwide economic downturn. Following a substantial drop in Wrath Arcane's sales, Bilovecky and DeBoe joined to create the Dredgers Union.

Positively Cleveland markets Greater Cleveland to vacation and business travelers. The area welcomes 14 million visitors annually who contribute about $4.5 billion dollars to the local economy. The Greater Cleveland Sports Commission, associated with Positively Cleveland and also residing on Fourth Street, both attracts and creates sports events for the Northeast Ohio region. The organization secured the International Children's Games (2004), NCAA Women's Final Four basketball tournament (2007), United States Figure Skating Championship (2009), a men's NCAA regional basketball tournament (2011), and the NCAA Women's Gymnastics Championship (2011), along with

collegiate and high school events involving football, hockey, soccer, wrestling, swimming, track, tennis, volleyball, and bowling. Major future events include the National Senior Games (2013) and Federation of Gay Games IX (2014).

As downtown Cleveland anticipates its new casino, medical mart, convention center, aquarium, office complex, hotels, and apartments, the city is primed to expand on the success of East Fourth Street, the first of the city's 21st Century triumphs.